CHEMISTRY F
TOMORROW'S W
SOLUTIONS MANUAL

Shea Mullally

Gill and Macmillan

Published in Ireland by
Gill and Macmillan Ltd
Goldenbridge
Dublin 8
with associated companies throughout the world

© Shea Mullally, 1991
© Artwork, Gill and Macmillan, 1991
0 7171 1902 5
Print origination in Ireland by
Datapage International Ltd

CONTENTS

CHAPTER 1.
ATOMIC STRUCTURE
AND THE PERIODIC
TABLE

(2)

Oxide 1 contains 4 g S and 4 g O; ratio 1 : 1; formula $= SO_2$ (32 g : 32 g)

Oxide 2 contains 3.2 g S and 12.8 g O; ratio 1 : 4; formula $= S_2O$ (64 g : 16 g)

Therefore, both conform to the law of multiple proportions.

(9)

% abundance	Fractional abundance	Isotope mass	Product
60.4	0.604	69	$69 \times 0.604 = 41.676$
39.6	0.396	71	$71 \times 0.396 = 28.116$
			Relative atomic mass $= 69.792$

The relative atomic mass, A_r, of gallium $= 69.7$

(10)

Element	% abundance	Fractional abundance	Isotope mass	Product
O	99.759	0.99759	16	$16 \times 0.99759 = 15.96144$
	0.037	0.00037	17	$17 \times 0.00037 = 0.00629$
	0.204	0.00204	18	$18 \times 0.00204 = 0.03672$
				$A_r(O) = 16.00445$

Element	% abundance	Fractional abundance	Isotope mass	Product
S	92.20	0.9220	28	$28 \times 0.9220 = 25.816$
	4.70	0.0470	29	$29 \times 0.0470 = 1.363$
	3.10	0.0310	30	$30 \times 0.0310 = 0.930$
				$A_r(S) = 28.109$

Element	% abundance	Fractional abundance	Isotope mass	Product
Mg	78.70	0.7870	24	$24 \times 0.7870 = 18.8880$
	10.13	0.1013	25	$25 \times 0.1013 = 2.5325$
	11.17	0.1117	26	$26 \times 0.1117 = 2.9042$
				$A_r(Mg) = 24.3247$

(11)

Element	Fractional abundance	Isotope mass	Product
Ir	0.373	191	$191 \times 0.373 = 71.243$
	0.627	193	$193 \times 0.627 = 121.011$

$$A_r(\text{Ir}) = 192.254$$

Element	Fractional abundance	Isotope mass	Product
Pb	0.015	204	$204 \times 0.015 = 3.600$
	0.236	206	$206 \times 0.236 = 48.616$
	0.226	207	$207 \times 0.226 = 46.782$
	0.523	208	$208 \times 0.523 = 108.784$

$$A_r(\text{Pb}) = 207.242$$

(14)

Let the % abundance of Li-6 $= a\%$
then the % abundance of Li-7 $= (100 - a)\%$
Therefore, in terms of fractional abundance

$$\frac{6 \times a}{100} + \frac{7 \times (100 - a)}{100} = 6.941$$

$$6a + 700 - 7a = 694.1$$
$$a = 5.9$$
$$100 - a = 94.1$$

(46)

If Cl—Cl bond distance	$= 198$ pm
then, atomic radius of Cl	$= 198$ pm$/2 = 99$ pm
As Cl—Br bond distance	$= 213$ pm
then, atomic radius of Br	$= (213 - 99)$ pm
	$= 114$ pm

(47)

Cl—Cl bond distance	$= 198$ pm
atomic radius of Cl	$= 99$ pm
Br—Cl bond distance	$= 213$ pm
atomic radius of Br	$= (213 - 99)$ pm $= 114$ pm
I—Br bond distance	$= 247$ pm
atomic radius of I	$= (247 - 114)$ pm $= 133$ pm
I—Cl bond distance	$=$ atomic radius of I $+$ atomic radius of Cl
	$= (133 + 99)$ pm
	$= 232$ pm

3

CHAPTER 2. AMOUNT OF SUBSTANCE—THE MOLE

(1)
(b)
(i)

$$M(CHCl_3) = (12.0 + 1.0 + 35.5 \times 3) \text{ g mol}^{-1}$$
$$= 119.5 \text{ g mol}^{-1}$$
$$M(KCl) = (39.1 + 35.5) \text{ g mol}^{-1}$$
$$= 74.6 \text{ g mol}^{-1}$$
$$M(Na^+) = 23.0 \text{ g mol}^{-1}$$
$$M(HCO_3^-) = (1.0 + 12.0 + 16.0 \times 3) \text{ g mol}^{-1}$$
$$= 61.0 \text{ g mol}^{-1}$$
$$M(Ca(OH)_2) = (40.1 + (16.0 + 1.0) \times 2) \text{ g mol}^{-1}$$
$$= 74.1 \text{ g mol}^{-1}$$
$$M(H) = 1.0 \text{ g mol}^{-1}$$
$$M(O_2) = (16.0 \times 2) \text{ g mol}^{-1}$$
$$= 32 \text{ g mol}^{-1}$$

(ii)

$$n = \frac{m}{M} = \frac{2 \text{ g NaOH}}{40.0 \text{ g mol}^{-1}} = 0.05 \text{ mol NaOH}$$

$$n = \frac{m}{M} = \frac{1.1 \text{ g CO}_2}{44.0 \text{ g mol}^{-1}} = 0.025 \text{ mol CO}_2$$

$$n = \frac{m}{M} = \frac{25 \text{ g CaCO}_3}{100.0 \text{ g mol}^{-1}} = 0.25 \text{ mol CaCO}_3$$

$$n = \frac{m}{M} = \frac{1 \text{ g H}}{1.0 \text{ g mol}^{-1}} = 1.0 \text{ mol H}$$

$$n = \frac{m}{M} = \frac{1 \text{ g H}}{2.0 \text{ g mol}^{-1}} = 0.5 \text{ mol H}_2$$

(iii)

$$m = nM = 2.5 \text{ mol} \times 399.1 \text{ g mol}^{-1} \text{ Fe}_2(SO_4)_3$$
$$= 999.75 \text{ g Fe}_2(SO_4)_3$$
$$m = nM = 0.5 \text{ mol} \times 17.0 \text{ g mol}^{-1} \text{ NH}_3$$
$$= 8.5 \text{ g NH}_3$$
$$m = nM = 2 \text{ mol} \times 23.0 \text{ g mol}^{-1} \text{ Na}$$
$$= 46.0 \text{ g Na}$$
$$m = nM = 0.1 \text{ mol} \times 63.5 \text{ g mol}^{-1} \text{ Cu}$$
$$= 6.35 \text{ g Cu}$$

(iv)

$N = nL = 2 \text{ mol} \times 6.022 \times 10^{23}$ HCl particles mol^{-1}
$\quad\quad\quad = 1.2044 \times 10^{24}$ HCl particles
$N = nL = 0.1 \text{ mol} \times 6.022 \times 10^{23}$ NaOH particles mol^{-1}
$\quad\quad\quad = 6.022 \times 10^{22}$ NaOH particles
$N = nL = 1.25 \text{ mol} \times 6.022 \times 10^{23}$ C particles mol^{-1}
$\quad\quad\quad = 7.5275 \times 10^{23}$ C particles

$$N = \frac{m}{M} L = \frac{2 \text{ g}}{2.0 \text{ g mol}^{-1}} \times 6.022 \times 10^{23} \text{ H}_2 \text{ particles mol}^{-1}$$

$$= 6.022 \times 10^{23} \text{ H}_2 \text{ particles}$$

$$N = \frac{m}{M} L = \frac{7 \text{ g}}{14.0 \text{ g mol}^{-1}} \times 6.022 \times 10^{23} \text{ N}_2 \text{ particles mol}^{-1}$$

$$= 3.011 \times 10^{23} \text{ N}_2 \text{ particles}$$

(v)

NaOH $\rightarrow$ Na$^+$ + OH$^-$
1 mol $\rightarrow$ 2 mol ions
0.25 $\rightarrow$ 0.5 mol ions

$$N = nL = 0.5 \text{ mol} \times 6.022 \times 10^{23} \text{ ions mol}^{-1}$$
$$= 3.011 \times 10^{23} \text{ ions}$$

CaCl$_2$ $\rightarrow$ Ca^{2+} + 2 Cl$^-$
1 mol $\rightarrow$ 3 mol ions
$\dfrac{37}{111}$ mol $\rightarrow$ 1 mol ions

$$N = nL = 1.0 \text{ mol} \times 6.022 \times 10^{23} \text{ ions mol}^{-1}$$
$$= 6.022 \times 10^{23} \text{ ions}$$

Ca$_3$(PO$_4$)$_2$ $\rightarrow$ 3 Ca^{2+} + 2 PO$_4{}^{3-}$
1 mol $\rightarrow$ 5 mol ions
2 mol $\rightarrow$ 10 mol ions

$$N = nL = 10.0 \text{ mol} \times 6.022 \times 10^{23} \text{ ions mol}^{-1}$$
$$= 6.022 \times 10^{24} \text{ ions}$$

(2)

$M(\text{N}_2) \quad = (14.0 \times 2) \text{ g mol}^{-1}$
$\quad\quad\quad\quad = 28.0 \text{ g mol}^{-1}$
$M(\text{CO}_2) \quad = (12.0 + 16.0 \times 2) \text{ g mol}^{-1}$
$\quad\quad\quad\quad = 44.0 \text{ g mol}^{-1}$
$M(\text{C}_2\text{H}_5\text{OH}) = (12.0 \times 2 + 1.0 \times 5 + 16.0 + 1.0) \text{ g mol}^{-1}$
$\quad\quad\quad\quad = 46.0 \text{ g mol}^{-1}$
$M(\text{SO}_4{}^{2-}) \quad = (32.1 + 16.0 \times 4) \text{ g mol}^{-1}$
$\quad\quad\quad\quad = 96.1 \text{ g mol}^{-1}$
$M(\text{Ca}) \quad = 40.1 \text{ g mol}^{-1}$

(3)

$$90 \text{ mg } C_6H_8O_6 = 0.09 \text{ g } C_6H_8O_6$$

$$N = \frac{m}{M}L = \frac{0.09 \text{ g}}{176.0 \text{ g mol}^{-1}} \times 6.022 \times 10^{23} \; C_6H_8O_6 \text{ molecules mol}^{-1}$$

$$= 3.079 \times 10^{20} \; C_6H_8O_6 \text{ molecules}$$

(4)

$$M + xs\ O_2 \rightarrow MO$$

$$0.972 \text{ g} \quad 0.64 \text{ g} \quad 1.612 \text{ g}$$

(a)

Amount of O_2,

$$n = \frac{m}{M} = \frac{0.64 \text{ g}}{32.0 \text{ g mol}^{-1}} = 0.02 \text{ mol}$$

(b)

Amount of metal $M = 2 \times$ amount $O_2 = 2 \times 0.02$ mol
$$= 0.04 \text{ mol}$$

Molar mass of metal $= \dfrac{m}{n} = \dfrac{0.972 \text{ g}}{0.04 \text{ mol}} = 24.3 \text{ g mol}^{-1}$

(5)

$$3 \text{ Fe} + 2 \text{ O}_2 \rightarrow \text{Fe}_3\text{O}_4$$

i.e. 3 mol Fe reacts with 2 mol O_2 to form 1 mol Fe_3O_4

$$n = \frac{m}{M} = \frac{21 \text{ g Fe}}{55.8 \text{ g mol}^{-1}} = 0.376 \text{ mol Fe}$$

$$n = \frac{m}{M} = \frac{16 \text{ g O}_2}{32.0 \text{ g mol}^{-1}} = 0.5 \text{ mol O}_2$$

According to the stoichiometric equation

(0.376/3) mol Fe reacts with $2 \times (0.376/2)$ mol O_2
0.125 mol Fe reacts with 0.25 mol O_2

As 0.5 mol $O_2 > 0.25$ mol O_2, then O_2 is in excess and Fe is the limiting reactant. Therefore,

$$0.376 \text{ mol Fe forms } 0.125 \text{ mol Fe}_3\text{O}_4$$

(6)
$S(s) + O_2(g) \quad\quad \rightarrow SO_2(g)$
$2 SO_2(g) + O_2(g) \rightarrow 2 SO_3(g)$
$SO_3(g) + H_2O(1) \rightarrow H_2SO_4(aq)$

The stoichiometric equations tell us that

$$1 \text{ mol S forms 1 mol SO}_2 \text{ which forms 1 mol H}_2\text{SO}_4$$

Therefore,

$$32 \text{ g S} \rightarrow 98 \text{ g H}_2\text{SO}_4$$

$$\frac{32 \times 2000 \text{ g}}{98} \text{ S} \rightarrow 2000 \text{ g H}_2\text{SO}_4$$

$$653.06 \text{ g S} \rightarrow 2000 \text{ g H}_2\text{SO}_4$$

Amount,

$$n = \frac{m}{M} = \frac{653 \text{ g}}{32 \text{ g mol}^{-1}} = 20.41 \text{ mol S}$$

(7)
(a)
$$2 \text{ Al(s)} + 3 \text{ I}_2(\text{s}) \rightarrow 2 \text{ AlI}_3(\text{s})$$
2 mol Al reacts with 3 mol I_2
1 mol Al reacts with 1.5 mol I_2

$$n = \frac{m}{M} = \frac{10.0 \text{ g}}{27.0 \text{ g mol}^{-1}} = 0.3704 \text{ mol Al}$$

Amount of $I_2 = 1.5 \times 0.3704$ mol I_2

Mass of I_2,
$$m = nM = 1.5 \times 0.3704 \text{ mol} \times 253.8 \text{ g mol}^{-1} \text{ I}_2$$
$$= 141.0 \text{ g I}_2$$

(b)

$$\text{Fe(s)} + \text{S(s)} \rightarrow \text{FeS(s)}$$

1 mol Fe reacts with 1 mol S

$$n = \frac{m}{M} = \frac{14.0 \text{ g}}{55.8 \text{ g mol}^{-1}} = 0.2509 \text{ mol Fe}$$

Amount of S = 0.2509 mol S
Mass of S,
$$m = nM = 0.2509 \text{ mol} \times 32.1 \text{ g mol}^{-1} \text{ S}$$
$$= 8.05 \text{ g S}$$

(c)

$$\%\text{N} = \frac{M(\text{N})}{M(\text{NH}_3)} \times 100\% = \frac{14.0 \text{ g mol}^{-1}}{17.0 \text{ g mol}^{-1}} \times 100\%$$
$$= 82.35\%$$

$$\%\text{N} = \frac{M(\text{N})}{M(\text{HNO}_3)} \times 100\% = \frac{14.0 \text{ g mol}^{-1}}{63.0 \text{ g mol}^{-1}} \times 100\%$$
$$= 22.22\%$$

$$\%\text{N} = \frac{2 \times M(\text{N})}{M(\text{NH}_4\text{NO}_3)} \times 100\% = \frac{2 \times 14.0 \text{ g mol}^{-1}}{80.0 \text{ g mol}^{-1}} \times 100\%$$
$$= 35\%$$

$$\%N = \frac{M(N)}{M(NO_2)} \times 100\% = \frac{14.0 \text{ g mol}^{-1}}{46.0 \text{ g mol}^{-1}} \times 100\%$$

$$= 30.43\%$$

$$\%N = \frac{2 \times M(N)}{M(N_2O_4)} \times 100\% = \frac{2 \times 14.0 \text{ g mol}^{-1}}{92.0 \text{ g mol}^{-1}} \times 100\%$$

$$= 30.43\%$$

$$\%N = \frac{2 \times M(N)}{M((NH_4)_2SO_4)} \times 100\% = \frac{2 \times 14.0 \text{ g mol}^{-1}}{132.0 \text{ g mol}^{-1}} \times 100\%$$

$$= 21.21\%$$

(8)
(i)

$$\%H_2O = \frac{10 \times M(H_2O)}{M(Na_2CO_3 \cdot 10H_2O)} \times 100\% = \frac{10 \times 18 \text{ g mol}^{-1}}{286 \text{ g mol}^{-1}} \times 100\%$$

$$= 62.94\%$$

(ii)

$$\%H_2O = \frac{5 \times M(H_2O)}{M(CuSO_4 \cdot 5H_2O)} \times 100\% = \frac{5 \times 18 \text{ g mol}^{-1}}{249.5 \text{ g mol}^{-1}} \times 100\%$$

$$= 36.07\%$$

(iii)

$$\%H_2O = \frac{7 \times M(H_2O)}{M(MgSO_4 \cdot 7H_2O)} \times 100\% = \frac{7 \times 18 \text{ g mol}^{-1}}{246.3 \text{ g mol}^{-1}} \times 100\%$$

$$= 51.16\%$$

(iv)

$$\%H_2O = \frac{24 \times M(H_2O)}{M(K_2SO_4 \cdot Al_2(SO_4)_3 \cdot 24H_2O)} \times 100\%$$

$$= \frac{24 \times 18.0 \text{ g mol}^{-1}}{948.2 \text{ g mol}^{-1}} \times 100\%$$

$$= 45.56\%$$

(9)

$2H_2S(g) + O_2(g) \rightarrow 2S(s) + 2H_2O(l)$

2 mol H_2S reacts with 1 mol O_2 to form 2 mol S

1 mol H_2S reacts with 0.5 mol O_2 to form 1 mol S

(a)

$$n = \frac{m}{M} = \frac{170.0 \text{ g}}{34.1 \text{ g mol}^{-1}} = 5.0 \text{ mol } H_2S$$

Amount of $O_2 = 0.5 \times 5.0 \text{ mol } O_2$

8

Mass of O_2,

$$m = nM = 0.5 \times 5.0 \text{ mol} \times 32.0 \text{ g mol}^{-1} O_2$$

$$= 80.0 \text{ g } O_2 = 0.08 \text{ kg } O_2$$

$$n = \frac{m}{M} = \frac{153000 \text{ g}}{34.1 \text{ g mol}^{-1}} = 4487 \text{ mol } H_2S$$

Amount of S formed = 4487 mol S
Mass of S,

$$m = nM = 4487 \text{ mol} \times 32.1 \text{ g mol}^{-1} S$$
$$= 14403 \text{ g S}$$

(10)
(a)

Constituent	Na	O
Mass/g	4.6	1.6
Molar mass/g mol^{-1}	23.0	16.0
Amount/mol	0.2	0.1
$\dfrac{\text{Amount}}{\text{Smallest amount}}$	$\dfrac{0.2}{0.1} = 2.0$	$\dfrac{0.1}{0.1} = 1.0$
Simplest ratio	2	1

Empirical formula = Na_2O

(b)

Constituent	C	H	N
Mass/g	48.8	13.5	37.7
Molar mass/g mol^{-1}	12.0	1.0	14.0
Amount/mol	4.07	13.5	2.7
$\dfrac{\text{Amount}}{\text{Smallest amount}}$	$\dfrac{4.07}{2.7} = 1.5$	$\dfrac{13.5}{2.7} = 5.0$	$\dfrac{2.7}{2.7} = 1.0$
Simplest ratio	3	10	2

Empirical formula = $C_3H_{10}N_2$

(c)

Constituent	C	H
Mass/g	90.0	10.0
Molar mass/g mol^{-1}	12.0	1.0
Amount/mol	7.5	10.0
$\dfrac{\text{Amount}}{\text{Smallest amount}}$	$\dfrac{7.5}{7.5} = 1.0$	$\dfrac{10.0}{7.5} = 1.33$
Simplest ratio	3	4

Empirical formula $= C_3H_4$

$$
\begin{aligned}
\text{Molecular formula} &= (\text{Empirical formula})_n \\
&= (C_3H_4)_n \\
&= (\{3 \times 12\} + \{4 \times 1\})_n \\
80 &= 40\,n \\
n &= 2
\end{aligned}
$$
Molecular formula $= C_6H_8$

(11)

$C_2H_2 + \frac{5}{2}O_2 \rightarrow 2CO_2 + H_2O$
1 mol   2.5 mol 2 mol   1 mol

(a)

$$n = \frac{m}{M} = \frac{52\ \text{g}}{26.0\ \text{g mol}^{-1}} = 2.0\ \text{mol}\ C_2H_2$$

Amount of O_2 which reacts $= 2.5 \times 2.0\ \text{mol}\ O_2 = 5.0\ \text{mol}\ O_2$

(b)

$$n = \frac{m}{M} = \frac{320\ \text{g}}{32.0\ \text{g mol}^{-1}} = 10.0\ \text{mol}\ O_2$$

$C_2H_2 + \frac{5}{2}O_2 \rightarrow 2CO_2 + H_2O$
1 mol C_2H_2 reacts with $\frac{5}{2}$ mol O_2
2 mol C_2H_2 reacts with 5 mol O_2
As $10.0 > 5.0$, then C_2H_2 is the limiting reactant.

(12)

$$
\begin{aligned}
\%\,\text{Yield} &= \frac{\text{Actual Yield}}{\text{Theoretical Yield}} \times 100\% \\[6pt]
&= \frac{24.1\ \text{g}}{34.54\ \text{g}} \times 100\% \\[6pt]
&= 69.77\%
\end{aligned}
$$

(13)

$$Zn(s) + 2HCl(aq) \rightarrow ZnCl_2(aq) + H_2(g)$$

1 mol Zn reacts with 2 mol HCl

0.15 mol Zn reacts with 0.30 mol HCl

As $1.04 > 0.30$, then Zn is the limiting reactant.

0.15 mol Zn reacts to produce 0.15 mol H_2

(14)

$$2Al(s) + 6HCl(g) \rightarrow 2AlCl_3(s) + 3H_2(g)$$

2 mol Al reacts with 6 mol HCl

0.30 mol Al reacts with 0.90 mol HCl

As 0.90 mol > 0.70 mol, then HCl is the limiting reactant.

$$0.70 \text{ mol HCl produces} \left(\frac{0.70}{3}\right) \text{mol AlCl}_3$$

i.e. 0.23 mol $AlCl_3$ are produced

(15)

$$2Al_2O_3 + 3C \rightarrow 4Al + 3CO_2$$

$$2 \text{ mol } Al_2O_3 \rightarrow 4 \text{ mol Al}$$

(a)

$$n = \frac{m}{M} = \frac{200 \text{ g}}{27.0 \text{ g mol}^{-1}} = 7.407 \text{ mol Al}$$

Amount of Al_2O_3 used $= 0.5 \times 7.407$ mol Al_2O_3

Mass of Al_2O_3 used,

$$m = nM = 0.5 \times 7.407 \text{ mol} \times 102 \text{ g mol}^{-1} Al_2O_3$$
$$= 377.76 \text{ g } Al_2O_3$$

(b)

$$1 \text{ kg ore} \rightarrow 500 \text{ g } Al_2O_3$$

$$n = \frac{m}{M} = \frac{500 \text{ g}}{102.0 \text{ g mol}^{-1}} = 4.902 \text{ mol } Al_2O_3$$

Amount of Al produced $= 2 \times 4.902$ mol Al

Mass of Al produced,

$$m = nM = 2 \times 4.902 \text{ mol} \times 27.0 \text{ g mol}^{-1} Al$$
$$= 264.71 \text{ g Al}$$

(c)

$$n = \frac{m}{M} = \frac{9 \times 10^5 \text{ g}}{102.0 \text{ g mol}^{-1}} = 8823.5 \text{ mol } Al_2O_3$$

$$n = \frac{m}{M} = \frac{2.4 \times 10^5 \text{ g}}{12.0 \text{ g mol}^{-1}} = 20000 \text{ mol C}$$

$2Al_2O_3 \quad + 3C \quad \rightarrow 4Al + 3CO_2$

1 mol $Al_2O_3 + \frac{3}{2}$ mol C $\rightarrow$ 2 mol Al

8823.5 mol Al_2O_3 reacts with 1.5×8823.5 mol C (132353.25 mol C)

As 20000 mol > 132353.25 mol, then Al_2O_3 is the limiting reactant.

Therefore, 88.2353 mol $Al_2O_3 \rightarrow 2 \times 8823.5$ mol C

Mass of Al produced,

$$m = nM = 2 \times 8823.5 \text{ mol} \times 27.0 \text{ g mol}^{-1} \text{ Al}$$
$$= 476469 \text{ g Al} = 476 \text{ kg Al}$$

(16)

$2CH_4(g) + O_2(g) + 4Cl_2(g) \rightarrow 8HCl(aq) + 2CO(g)$

2 mol CH_4 reacts with 4 mol Cl_2 (O_2 is in excess)

$$n = \frac{m}{M} = \frac{26.0 \text{ g}}{16.0 \text{ g mol}^{-1}} = 1.625 \text{ mol } CH_4$$

$$n = \frac{m}{M} = \frac{130.0 \text{ g}}{71.0 \text{ g mol}^{-1}} = 1.831 \text{ mol } Cl_2$$

1.625 mol CH_4 reacts with 3.25 mol Cl_2

As $1.831 < 3.25$, then Cl_2 is the limiting reactant.

$$4 \text{ mol } Cl_2 \quad \rightarrow 8 \text{ mol HCl}$$
$$1.831 \text{ mol } Cl_2 \rightarrow 3.662 \text{ mol HCl}$$

Theoretical mass of HCl produced, $m = nM = 3.662 \text{ mol} \times 36.5 \text{ g mol}^{-1} \text{ HCl}$
$$= 133.66 \text{ g HCl}$$

$$\% \text{ Yield} = \frac{\text{Actual Yield}}{\text{Theoretical Yield}} \times 100\%$$

$$= \frac{116.0 \text{ g}}{133.66 \text{ g}} \times 100\%$$

$$= 86.8\% \text{ HCl}$$

(18)
(a)

$$c = \frac{n}{V} = \frac{1.0 \text{ mol NaOH}}{2.0 \text{ dm}^3} = 0.5 \text{ mol dm}^{-3} \text{ NaOH}$$

$$c = \frac{n}{V} = \frac{0.1 \text{ mol Na}_2\text{CO}_3}{0.25 \text{ dm}^3} = 0.4 \text{ mol dm}^{-3} \text{ Na}_2\text{CO}_3$$

$$c = \frac{n}{V} = \frac{0.1 \text{ mol HCl}}{0.5 \text{ dm}^3} = 0.2 \text{ mol dm}^{-3} \text{ HCl}$$

$$c = \frac{n}{V} = \frac{0.25 \text{ mol H}_2\text{SO}_4}{5.0 \text{ dm}^3}a = 0.05 \text{ mol dm}^{-3} \text{ H}_2\text{SO}_4$$

(b)

Rearranging $c = \frac{n}{V}$ and $n = \frac{m}{M}$

$$c = \frac{m}{MV} = \frac{20.0 \text{ g NaOH}}{40.0 \text{ g mol}^{-1} \times 0.25 \text{ dm}^3} = 2.0 \text{ mol dm}^{-3} \text{ NaOH}$$

$$c = \frac{m}{MV} = \frac{13.1 \text{ g Na}_2\text{Cr}_2\text{O}_7}{262.0 \text{ g mol}^{-1} \times 0.5 \text{ dm}^3} = 0.1 \text{ mol dm}^{-3} \text{ Na}_2\text{Cr}_2\text{O}_7$$

$$c = \frac{m}{MV} = \frac{3.65 \text{ g HCl}}{36.5 \text{ g mol}^{-1} \times 1.0 \text{ dm}^3} = 0.1 \text{ mol dm}^{-3} \text{ HCl}$$

$$c = \frac{m}{MV} = \frac{4.9 \text{ g H}_2\text{SO}_4}{98.0 \text{ g mol}^{-1} \times 0.5 \text{ dm}^3} = 0.1 \text{ mol dm}^{-3} \text{ H}_2\text{SO}_4$$

(19)

$n = cV = 2.5 \text{ mol dm}^{-3} \times 2.0 \text{ dm}^3 \text{ NaOH} = 5.0 \text{ mol NaOH}$
$n = cV = 0.5 \text{ mol dm}^{-3} \times 0.3 \text{ dm}^3 \text{ HCl} = 0.15 \text{ mol HCl}$
$n = cV = 2.0 \text{ mol dm}^{-3} \times 0.05 \text{ dm}^3 \text{ H}_2\text{SO}_4 = 0.1 \text{ mol H}_2\text{SO}_4$

(20)
(i)

$n = cV = 0.25 \text{ mol dm}^{-3} \times 0.25 \text{ dm}^3 \text{ NaOH} = 0.0625 \text{ mol NaOH}$
$m = nM = 0.0625 \text{ mol} \times 40 \text{ g mol}^{-1} \text{ NaOH} = 2.5 \text{ g NaOH}$

(ii)

$n = cV = 0.5 \text{ mol dm}^{-3} \times 0.1 \text{ dm}^3 \text{ HCl} = 0.05 \text{ mol HCl}$

$$V = \frac{n}{c} = \frac{0.05 \text{ mol HCl}}{10.0 \text{ mol dm}^{-3}} = 0.005 \text{ dm}^3 \text{ HCl} = 5 \text{ cm}^3 \text{ HCl}$$

i.e. 5 cm^3 of 10.0 mol dm^{-3} HCl in 100 cm^3 of solution.

(iii)

$n = cV = 0.1 \text{ mol dm}^{-3} \times 0.2 \text{ dm}^3 \text{ Na}_2\text{CO}_3 = 0.02 \text{ mol Na}_2\text{CO}_3$

$m = nM = 0.02 \text{ mol} \times 106 \text{ g mol}^{-1} \text{ Na}_2\text{CO}_3 = 2.12 \text{ g Na}_2\text{CO}_3$

(iv)
20 cm^3 of 100% w/v H$_2$O$_2$ in 100 cm^3 solution = 20% w/v H$_2$O$_2$

(v)
10 g sucrose in 100 cm^3 of solution = 10% w/v sucrose solution

(vi)
25 cm^3 methanol + 75 cm^3 ethanol = 25% v/v methanol in ethanol

(vii)
25 mg CaCO$_3$ dm^{-3} = 25 ppm CaCO$_3$

$$HCl + NaOH \rightarrow NaCl + H_2O$$

$$\frac{c_A V_A}{a} = \frac{c_B V_B}{b}$$

$$\frac{0.1 \text{ mol dm}^{-3} \times 100 \text{ cm}^3}{1} = \frac{0.2 \text{ mol dm}^{-3} \times V_B}{1}$$

$$V_B = 50 \text{ cm}^3 \text{ NaOH}$$

$$H_2SO_4 + 2NaOH \rightarrow Na_2SO_4 + 2H_2O$$

$$\frac{c_A V_A}{a} = \frac{c_B V_B}{b}$$

$$\frac{0.2 \text{ mol dm}^{-3} \times 300 \text{ cm}^3}{1} = \frac{0.2 \text{ mol dm}^{-3} \times V_B}{2}$$

$$V_B = 600 \text{ cm}^3 \text{ NaOH}$$

$$HNO_3 + NaOH \rightarrow NaNO_3 + H_2O$$

$$\frac{c_A V_A}{a} = \frac{c_B V_B}{b}$$

$$\frac{0.4 \text{ mol dm}^{-3} \times 1 \text{ dm}^3}{1} = \frac{0.2 \text{ mol dm}^{-3} \times V_B}{1}$$

$$V_B = 2 \text{ dm}^3 \text{ NaOH}$$

$$HNO_3 + NaOH \rightarrow NaNO_3 + H_2O$$

$$\frac{c_A V_A}{a} = \frac{c_B V_B}{b}$$

$$\frac{2.5 \text{ mol dm}^{-3} \times 25 \text{ cm}^3}{1} = \frac{0.2 \text{ mol dm}^{-3} \times V_B}{1}$$

$$V_B = 312.5 \text{ cm}^3 \text{ NaOH}$$

$$CH_3COOH + NaOH \rightarrow CH_3COONa + H_2O$$

$$\frac{c_A V_A}{a} = \frac{c_B V_B}{b}$$

$$\frac{1.0 \text{ mol dm}^{-3} \times 50 \text{ cm}^3}{1} = \frac{0.2 \text{ mol dm}^{-3} \times V_B}{1}$$

$$V_B = 250 \text{ cm}^3 \text{ NaOH}$$

$$HCl + NaOH \rightarrow NaCl + H_2O$$

$$\frac{c_A V_A}{a} = \frac{c_B V_B}{b}$$

$$\frac{0.01 \text{ mol dm}^{-3} \times 2.5 \text{ dm}^3}{1} = \frac{0.2 \text{ mol dm}^{-3} \times V_B}{1}$$

$$V_B = 125 \text{ cm}^3$$

(23)
1.29 g Mg^{2+} ion in 1 kg of water = 1290 mg dm^{-3} = 1290 ppm

(24)
(a)
 0.021 mg Cd^{2+} in 5.0 dm^3 of water = 0.0042 mg Cd^{2+} dm^{-3} = 0.0042 ppm Cd^{2+}

As 0.0042 ppm < 0.01 ppm, the concentration of cadmium in the water does not contravene the health regulations.

(b)

$$0.40 \text{ g } CO_2 \text{ in } 2.5 \text{ dm}^3 = 160 \text{ mg } CO_2 \text{ dm}^{-3} = 160 \text{ ppm } CO_2$$

As 160 ppm < 200 ppm, the concentration of carbon dioxide in the water does not contravene the health regulations.

(25)
(a)
20% w/v ethanol = 20 g ethanol in 100 g solution
$\qquad\qquad\qquad\quad$ = 20 g ethanol in 126 cm^3 solution

$$c = \frac{m}{MV} = \frac{20.0 \text{ g}}{46.0 \text{ g mol}^{-1} \times 0.126 \text{ dm}^3}$$

$$= 3.45 \text{ mol dm}^{-3} \text{ ethanol}$$

(b)
40% w/v ethanol = 40 g ethanol in 100 cm^3 solution

$$c = \frac{m}{MV} = \frac{40.0 \text{ g}}{46.0 \text{ g mol}^{-1} \times 0.1 \text{ dm}^3}$$

$$= 8.70 \text{ mol dm}^{-3} \text{ ethanol}$$

(26)

$$HCl + NaOH \rightarrow NaCl + H_2O$$

$$\frac{c_A V_A}{a} = \frac{c_B V_B}{b}$$

$$\frac{0.1 \text{ mol dm}^{-3} \times 21.5 \text{ cm}^3}{1} = \frac{c_B \times 25.0 \text{ cm}^3}{1}$$

$$c_B = 0.086 \text{ mol dm}^{-3} \text{ NaOH}$$

$$= 0.086 \text{ mol dm}^{-3} \times 40.0 \text{ g mol}^{-1} \text{ NaOH}$$

$$= 3.44 \text{ g dm}^{-3} \text{ NaOH}$$

(27)

$$\text{Mean titre} = \frac{22.45 + 22.50 + 22.55}{3} \text{ cm}^3 \text{ HCl}$$

$$= 22.50 \text{ cm}^3 \text{ HCl}$$

$$\text{HCl} + \text{NaOH} \rightarrow \text{NaCl} + \text{H}_2\text{O}$$

$$\frac{c_A V_A}{a} = \frac{c_B V_B}{b}$$

$$\frac{c_A \times 22.50 \text{ cm}^3}{1} = \frac{0.23 \text{ mol dm}^{-3} \times 25.0 \text{ cm}^3}{1}$$

$$c_A = 0.255 \text{ mol dm}^{-3} \text{ HCl}$$

(28)

$$c = \frac{m}{MV} = \frac{3.60 \text{ g NaHCO}_3}{84.0 \text{ g mol}^{-1} \times 1.0 \text{ dm}^3} = 0.0429 \text{ mol dm}^{-3}$$

$$\text{NaHCO}_3(\text{aq}) + \text{HCl}(\text{aq}) \rightarrow \text{NaCl}(\text{aq}) + \text{CO}_2(\text{g}) + \text{H}_2\text{O}(\text{l})$$

$$\frac{c_A V_A}{a} = \frac{c_B V_B}{b}$$

$$\frac{0.0429 \text{ mol dm}^{-3} \times 25 \text{ cm}^3}{1} = \frac{c_B \times 22.50 \text{ cm}^3}{1}$$

$$c_B = 0.0478 \text{ mol dm}^{-3} \text{ HCl}$$

$$= 0.0478 \text{ mol dm}^{-3} \times 36.5 \text{ g mol}^{-1} \text{ HCl}$$

$$= 1.7447 \text{ g dm}^{-3} \text{ HCl}$$

(29)

$$\text{Na}_2\text{CO}_3(\text{aq}) + 2\text{HCl}(\text{aq}) \rightarrow 2\text{NaCl}(\text{aq}) + \text{CO}_2(\text{g}) + \text{H}_2\text{O}(\text{l})$$

$$\frac{c_A V_A}{a} = \frac{c_B V_B}{b}$$

$$\frac{c_A \times 25 \text{ cm}^3}{1} = \frac{0.2 \text{ mol dm}^{-3} \times 15.0 \text{ cm}^3}{2}$$

$$c_A = 0.06 \text{ mol dm}^{-3} \text{ Na}_2\text{CO}_3$$

$$= 0.03 \text{ mol Na}_2\text{CO}_3/500 \text{ cm}^3 \text{ solution}$$

$$= 0.03 \text{ mol} \times 106 \text{ g mol}^{-1} \text{ Na}_2\text{CO}_3/500 \text{ cm}^3 \text{ solution}$$

$$= 3.18 \text{ g Na}_2\text{CO}_3/500 \text{ cm}^3 \text{ solution}$$

Mass of water of crystallisation $= 8.6 \text{ g} - 3.18 \text{ g} = 5.42 \text{ g H}_2\text{O}$

$\%$ water in crystals $= \dfrac{5.42 \text{ g}}{8.6 \text{ g}} \times 100\%$ $\qquad = 63.0\%$

16

Amount of water of crystallisation, $n = \dfrac{m}{M} = \dfrac{5.42 \text{ g}}{18.0 \text{ g mol}^{-1}}$

$$= 0.3011 \text{ mol H}_2\text{O}$$

$$x = \frac{\text{Amount of H}_2\text{O}}{\text{Amount of Na}_2\text{CO}_3} = \frac{0.3011 \text{ mol}}{0.03 \text{ mol}} = 10$$

(30)
Amount of unreacted HCl

$$\text{HCl} + \text{NaOH} \rightarrow \text{NaCl} + \text{H}_2\text{O}$$

$$\frac{c_A V_A}{a} = \frac{c_B V_B}{b}$$

$$\frac{c_A \times 25.0 \text{ cm}^3}{1} = \frac{1.0 \text{ mol dm}^{-3} \times 24.1 \text{ cm}^3}{1}$$

$$c_A = 0.964 \text{ mol dm}^{-3} \text{ HCl}$$

Amount of unreacted HCl,
$$n = cV = 0.964 \text{ mol dm}^{-3} \text{ HCl} \times 0.25 \text{ dm}^3$$
$$= 0.241 \text{ mol HCl}$$

Amount of HCl initially,

$$n = cV = 5.0 \text{ mol dm}^{-3} \text{ HCl} \times 0.05 \text{ dm}^3$$
$$= 0.25 \text{ mol HCl}$$

Amount of HCl which reacted with Mg(OH)_2

$$= \text{Amount of HCl initially} - \text{Amount of unreacted HCl}$$
$$= (0.25 - 0.241) \text{ mol HCl} = 0.009 \text{ mol HCl}$$

$$2 \text{ HCl} + \text{Mg(OH)}_2 \rightarrow \text{MgCl}_2 + 2\text{H}_2\text{O}$$

$$2 \text{ mol HCl reacts with 1 mol Mg(OH)}_2$$

$$0.009 \text{ mol reacts with } 0.0045 \text{ mol Mg(OH)}_2$$

$$m = nM = 0.0045 \text{ mol} \times 58.3 \text{ g mol}^{-1} \text{ Mg(OH)}_2$$
$$= 0.26235 \text{ g Mg(OH)}_2$$

% Mg(OH)_2 in the 'milk of magnesia' tablet

$$= \frac{\text{Mass of Mg(OH)}_2}{\text{Mass of tablet}} \times 100\%$$

$$= \frac{0.26235 \text{ g}}{0.4 \text{ g}} \times 100\% = 65.6\%$$

(31)
Amount of unreacted HCl

$$HCl + NaOH \rightarrow NaCl + H_2O$$

$$\frac{c_A V_A}{a} = \frac{c_B V_B}{b}$$

$$\frac{c_A \times 25.0 \text{ cm}^3}{1} = \frac{0.1 \text{ mol dm}^{-3} \times 21.0 \text{ cm}^3}{1}$$

$$c_A = 0.084 \text{ mol dm}^{-3} \text{ HCl}$$

Amount of unreacted HCl,
$$n = cV = 0.084 \text{ mol dm}^{-3} \text{ HCl} \times 0.25 \text{ dm}^3$$
$$= 0.021 \text{ mol HCl}$$

Amount of HCl initially,
$$n = cV = 1.0 \text{ mol dm}^{-3} \text{ HCl} \times 0.05 \text{ dm}^3$$
$$= 0.05 \text{ mol HCl}$$

Amount of HCl which reacted with $CaCO_3$
$$= \text{Amount of HCl initially} - \text{Amount of unreacted HCl}$$
$$= (0.05 - 0.021) \text{ mol HCl} = 0.029 \text{ mol HCl}$$

$$2HCl + CaCO_3 \rightarrow CaCl_2 + 2H_2O$$

2 mol HCl reacts with 1 mol $CaCO_3$

0.029 mol HCl reacts with 0.0145 mol $CaCO_3$

$$m = nM = 0.0145 \text{ mol} \times 100 \text{ g mol}^{-1} \text{ CaCO}_3$$
$$= 1.45 \text{ g CaCO}_3$$

$\% \text{CaCO}_3$ in the limestone

$$= \frac{\text{Mass of CaCO}_3}{\text{Mass of limestone}} \times 100\%$$

$$= \frac{1.45 \text{ g}}{1.6 \text{ g}} \times 100\% = 90.825\% = 91\%$$

(32)
Amount of unreacted NaOH

$$H_2SO_4 + 2NaOH \rightarrow Na_2SO_4 + 2H_2O$$

$$\frac{c_A V_A}{a} = \frac{c_B V_B}{b}$$

$$\frac{0.05 \text{ mol dm}^{-3} \times 12.4 \text{ cm}^3}{1} = \frac{c_B \times 25.0 \text{ cm}^3}{2}$$

$$c_B = 0.0496 \text{ mol dm}^{-3} \text{ NaOH}$$

Amount of unreacted NaOH,
$$n = cV = 0.0496 \text{ mol dm}^{-3} \text{ NaOH} \times 0.25 \text{ dm}^3$$
$$= 0.0124 \text{ mol NaOH}$$

Amount of NaOH initially,
$$n = cV = 0.5 \text{ mol dm}^{-3} \text{ HCl} \times 0.05 \text{ dm}^3$$
$$= 0.025 \text{ mol NaOH}$$

Amount of NaOH which reacted with H_2SO_4
= Amount of NaOH initially − Amount of unreacted NaOH
= (0.025 − 0.0124) mol NaOH = 0.0126 mol NaOH

$$CH_3COOC_6H_4COOH + 2NaOH \rightarrow CH_3COONa + HOC_5H_4COONa$$

1 mol $CH_3COOC_6H_4COOH$ reacts with 2 mol NaOH
0.0063 mol $CH_3COOC_6H_4COOH$ reacts with 0.0126 mol NaOH

$$m = nM = 0.0063 \text{ mol} \times 180.0 \text{ g mol}^{-1} \, CH_3COOC_6H_4COOH$$

$$= 1.134 \text{ g } CH_3COOC_6H_4COOH$$

6% $CH_3COOC_6H_4COOH$ in the aspirin tablet

$$= \frac{\text{Mass of } CH_3COOC_6H_4COOH}{\text{Mass of tablet}} \times 100\%$$

$$= \frac{1.134 \text{ g}}{1.5 \text{ g}} \times 100\% = 75.6\%$$

CHAPTER 3.
PARTICLES IN MOTION AND THE GASEOUS STATE

(6)
(i)
1 mol of dry air contains

$$0.78 \text{ mol } N_2, 0.21 \text{ mol } O_2, 0.095 \text{ mol Ar}, 0.005 \text{ mol } CO_2$$

(ii)

$$
\begin{aligned}
m &= nM = 0.78 \text{ mol} \times 14.0 \text{ g mol}^{-1} \, N_2 &&= 10.92 \text{ g } N_2 \\
m &= nM = 0.21 \text{ mol} \times 32.0 \text{ g mol}^{-1} \, O_2 &&= 6.72 \text{ g } O_2 \\
m &= nM = 0.095 \text{ mol} \times 39.9 \text{ g mol}^{-1} \, N_2 &&= 3.80 \text{ g } N_2 \\
m &= nM = 0.005 \text{ mol} \times 44.0 \text{ g mol}^{-1} \, CO_2 &&= 0.22 \text{ g } N_2
\end{aligned}
$$

(7)

$$\frac{\text{Rate 1}}{\text{Rate 2}} = \sqrt{\frac{M_2}{M_1}} = \sqrt{\frac{64}{44}}$$

i.e. gases diffuse in the ratio $6.63 : 8$

(8)

$$\text{Rate (Helium)} = \frac{\text{Volume}}{\text{Time}} = \frac{10 \text{ cm}^3}{7.04 \text{ s}}$$

$$\text{Rate (Oxygen)} = \frac{\text{Volume}}{\text{Time}} = \frac{10 \text{ cm}^3}{X \text{ s}}$$

Applying Graham's law,

$$\frac{\text{Rate 1}}{\text{Rate 2}} = \sqrt{\frac{M_2}{M_1}}$$

$$\frac{10 \text{ cm}^3}{7.04 \text{ s}} \times \frac{X}{10 \text{ cm}^3} = \sqrt{\frac{32}{4}}$$

$$\frac{X}{7.04} = \sqrt{8} \text{ s}$$

$$X = 7.04 \times \sqrt{8} \text{ s} = 19.9 \text{ s}$$

(12)
(b)

$$p_1 V_1 = p_2 V_2$$
$$97 \text{ kPa} \times 200 \text{ cm}^3 = 104 \text{ kPa} \times V_2$$
$$V_2 = 186.54 \text{ cm}^3$$

(c)

$$\frac{V_1}{T_1} = \frac{V_2}{T_2}$$

$$\frac{450 \text{ cm}^3}{300 \text{ K}} = \frac{V_2}{310 \text{ K}}$$

$$V_2 = 465 \text{ cm}^3$$

(13)

$$p_1 V_1 = p_2 V_2$$
$$10^5 \text{ Pa} \times 2.5 \text{ dm}^3 = p_2 \times 10.5 \text{ dm}^3$$
$$p_2 = 2.38 \times 10^4 \text{ Pa}$$

(14)
(a)

$$\frac{V_1}{T_1} = \frac{V_2}{T_2}$$

$$\frac{3.5 \text{ dm}^3}{288 \text{ K}} = \frac{V_2}{303 \text{ K}}$$

$$V_2 = 3.68 \text{ dm}^3$$

$$\frac{V_1}{T_1} = \frac{V_2}{T_2}$$

$$\frac{3.5 \text{ dm}^3}{288 \text{ K}} = \frac{V_2}{280.5 \text{ K}}$$

$$V_2 = 3.41 \text{ dm}^3$$

(15)

$$NH_4Cl(s) \rightarrow NH_3(g) + HCl(g)$$

Amount of NH_4Cl, $n = \dfrac{m}{M} = \dfrac{10 \text{ g}}{53.5 \text{ g mol}^{-1}} = 0.187 \text{ mol } NH_4Cl$

As $1 \text{ mol } NH_4Cl(s) \rightarrow 1 \text{ mol } NH_3(g) + 1 \text{ mol } HCl(g)$
then $0.187 \text{ mol } NH_4Cl \rightarrow 2 \times 0.187 \text{ mol gas} = 0.374 \text{ mol gas}$

$$pV = nRT \quad \text{is rearranged to} \quad V = \frac{nRT}{p}$$

Therefore,

$$V = \frac{0.374 \text{ mol} \times 8.314 \text{ J K}^{-1} \text{mol}^{-1} \times 873 \text{ K}}{10^5 \text{ Nm}^{-2}}$$

$$= 2.715 \times 10^{-2} \text{ JN}^{-1} \text{m}^2 = 2.715 \times 10^{-2} \text{ Nm N}^{-1} \text{m}^2 (1 \text{ J} = 1 \text{ Nm})$$

$$= 2.715 \times 10^{-2} \text{ m}^3$$

$$= 27.15 \text{ dm}^3$$

(16)
(a)

$$\frac{p_1 V_1}{T_1} = \frac{p_2 V_2}{T_2}$$

$$\frac{103 \text{ kPa} \times 40 \text{ cm}^3}{303 \text{ K}} = \frac{99 \text{ kPa} \times V_2}{293 \text{ K}}$$

$$V_2 = 40.2 \text{ cm}^3$$

$$\frac{p_1 V_1}{T_1} = \frac{p_2 V_2}{T_2}$$

$$\frac{102 \text{ kPa} \times 280 \text{ cm}^3}{300 \text{ K}} = \frac{p_2 \times 250 \text{ cm}^3}{294 \text{ K}}$$

$$p_2 = 112 \text{ kPa}$$

(17)

$$\frac{p_1 V_1}{T_1} = \frac{p_2 V_2}{T_2}$$

$$\frac{10^5 \text{ Pa} \times 1.0 \text{ dm}^3}{298 \text{ K}} = \frac{p_2 \times 0.0714 \text{ dm}^3}{773 \text{ K}}$$

$$p_2 = 3.63 \times 10^6 \text{ Pa}$$

(18)

$$CaCO_3(s) + 2HCl(aq) \rightarrow CaCl(aq) + CO_2(g) + H_2O(1)$$

Amount of $CaCO_3$,

$$n = \frac{m}{M} = \frac{150 \text{ g}}{100 \text{ g mol}^{-1}} = 1.5 \text{ mol CaCO}_3$$

$$1 \text{ mol CaCO}_3(s) \rightarrow 1 \text{ mol CO}_2(g)$$

$$1.5 \text{ mol CaCO}_3(s) \rightarrow 1.5 \text{ mol CO}_2(g)$$

$$V = nV_m \text{ at STP}$$

$$= 1.5 \times 22.4 \text{ dm}^3 \text{ CO}_2 \text{ at STP}$$

$$= 33.6 \text{ dm}^3 \text{ CO}_2 \text{ at STP}$$

(b)

The equation of state

$$pV = nRT \quad \text{is rearranged to} \quad V = \frac{nRT}{p}$$

Therefore,

$$V = \frac{1.5 \text{ mol} \times 8.314 \text{ JK}^{-1} \text{ mol}^{-1} \times 323 \text{ K}}{2 \times 10^5 \text{ Nm}^{-2}}$$

$$= 2.014 \times 10^{-1} \text{ JN}^{-1} \text{ m}^2 = 2.014 \times 10^{-1} \text{ Nm N}^{-1} \text{ m}^2 (1 \text{ J} = 1 \text{ Nm})$$

$$= 2.014 \times 10^{-1} \text{ m}^3$$

$$= 201.4 \text{ dm}^3$$

(19)

$$4FeS_2(s) + 11O_2(g) \rightarrow Fe_2O_3(s) + 8SO_2(g)$$

Amount of FeS_2,

$$n = \frac{m}{M} = \frac{200 \text{ g}}{120 \text{ g mol}^{-1}} = 1.67 \text{ mol FeS}_2$$

$$4 \text{ mol FeS}_2 \quad \rightarrow 8 \text{ mol SO}_2(g)$$

$$1.67 \text{ mol FeS}_2 \rightarrow 3.33 \text{ mol SO}_2(g)$$

$$V = nV_m \text{ at STP}$$

$$= 3.33 \times 22.4 \text{ dm}^3 \text{ SO}_2 \text{ at STP}$$

$$= 74.66 \text{ dm}^3 \text{ SO}_2 \text{ at STP}$$

(20)
(b)

$$n = \frac{V}{V_m} = \frac{0.2 \text{ dm}^3}{22.4 \text{ dm}^3 \text{ mol}^{-1}} = 8.93 \times 10^{-3} \text{ mol O}_2$$

(e)
Amount of N_2,

$$n = \frac{m}{M} = \frac{2.0 \text{ g}}{28.0 \text{ g mol}^{-1}} = 0.071 \text{ mol N}_2$$

The equation of state

$$pV = nRT \quad \text{is rearranged to} \quad V = \frac{nRT}{p}$$

Therefore,

$$V = \frac{0.071 \text{ mol} \times 8.314 \text{ JK}^{-1} \text{ mol}^{-1} \times 283 \text{ K}}{70000 \text{ Nm}^{-2}}$$

$$= 2.38 \times 10^{-3} \text{ JN}^{-1} \text{ m}^2 = 2.38 \times 10^{-3} \text{ Nm N}^{-1} \text{ m}^2 (1 \text{ J} = 1 \text{ Nm})$$

$$= 2.38 \times 10^{-3} \text{ m}^3$$

$$= 2.38 \text{ dm}^3$$

(f)

The equation of state

$$pV = nRT \quad \text{is rearranged to } n = \frac{pV}{RT}$$

Therefore, the amount, $n = \dfrac{150000 \text{ Nm}^{-2} \times 0.1 \text{ m}^3}{8.314 \text{ JK}^{-1} \text{ mol}^{-1} \times 300 \text{ K}}$

$$= \frac{150000 \times 0.1 \text{ Nm}}{8.314 \times 300 \text{ J mol}^{-1}}$$

$$= \frac{150000 \times 0.1 \text{ J}}{8.314 \times 300 \text{ J mol}^{-1}}$$

$$= 6.0 \text{ mol H}_2$$

Now, mass, $m = nM = 6.0 \text{ mol} \times 2 \text{ g mol}^{-1} \text{ H}_2$
$$= 12.0 \text{ g H}_2$$

(21)

$$HC(g) + O_2 \rightarrow H_2O(g) + CO_2(g)$$

$$30 \text{ cm}^3 \text{ HC} + 150 \text{ cm}^3 \text{ O}_2 \rightarrow 90 \text{ cm}^3 \text{ CO}_2$$

Dividing each volume by V_m (22.4 dm³)

$$1.339 \text{ mol HC} + 6.696 \text{ mol O}_2 \rightarrow 4.017 \text{ mol CO}_2$$

$$1 \text{ mol HC} \quad + 5 \text{ mol O}_2 \quad \rightarrow 3 \text{ mol CO}_2$$

i.e. $HC(g) \quad + 5 O_2 \quad \rightarrow 3CO_2(g) + 4H_2O(g)$

Therefore, the formula of HC is C_3H_8 (propane).

(22)

The equation of state

$$pV = nRT \quad \text{is rearranged to } n = \frac{pV}{RT}$$

Therefore, the amount, $n = \dfrac{0.95 \times 10^5 \text{ Nm}^{-2} \times 6.0 \times 10^3 \text{ m}^3}{8.314 \text{ JK}^{-1} \text{ mol}^{-1} \times 300 \text{ K}}$

$$= 2.29 \times 10^5 \text{ mol He}$$

Mass of He, $m = nM = 2.285 \times 10^5 \text{ mol} \times 4.0 \text{ g mol}^{-1} \text{ He}$

$$= 9.14 \times 10^5 \text{ g He}$$

(23)
The equation of state

$$pV = nRT \quad \text{is rearranged to} \quad n = \frac{pV}{RT}$$

Therefore, the amount, $n = \dfrac{10^5 \, \text{Nm}^{-2} \times 4.15 \times 10^{-4} \, \text{m}^3}{8.314 \, \text{JK}^{-1} \, \text{mol}^{-1} \times 373 \, \text{K}}$

$$= 0.0134 \, \text{mol}$$

Molar mass, $M = \dfrac{m}{n} = \dfrac{0.63 \, \text{g}}{0.0134 \, \text{mol}} = 47.01 \, \text{g mol}^{-1}$

$$M(C_2H_5OH) = 46.0 \, \text{g mol}^{-1}$$

(24)
The equation of state

$$pV = nRT \quad \text{is rearranged to} \quad n = \frac{pV}{RT}$$

The amount of propanone, $n = \dfrac{101 \times 10^3 \, \text{Nm}^{-2} \times 6.15 \times 10^{-5} \, \text{m}^3}{8.314 \, \text{JK}^{-1} \, \text{mol}^{-1} \times 373 \, \text{K}}$

$$= 2.003 \times 10^{-3} \, \text{mol propanone}$$

Molar mass, $M = \dfrac{m}{n} = \dfrac{0.10 \, \text{g}}{2.003 \times 10^{-3} \, \text{mol}} = 49.9 \, \text{g mol}^{-1}$

$$M(CH_3COCH_3) = 58.0 \, \text{g mol}^{-1}$$

(25)
Total pressure, $p = p_{O_2} + p_{He} + p_{N_2}$

$$125 \, \text{kPa} = 30 \, \text{kPa} + 45 \, \text{kPa} + p_{N_2}$$

Therefore $p_{N_2} = 50 \, \text{kPa}$

$$p_{O_2} = \frac{30 \, \text{kPa}}{125 \, \text{kPa}} = 0.24$$

$$p_{He} = \frac{45 \, \text{kPa}}{125 \, \text{kPa}} = 0.36$$

$$p_{N_2} = \frac{50 \, \text{kPa}}{125 \, \text{kPa}} = 0.40$$

(26)

$$\frac{p_1 V_1}{T_1} = \frac{p_2 V_2}{T_2}$$

$$\frac{100 \text{ kPa} \times 6.0 \text{ dm}^3}{288 \text{ K}} = \frac{80 \text{ kPa} \times V_2}{293 \text{ K}}$$

$$V_2 = 7.63 \text{ cm}^3$$

(27)

$$\frac{p_1 V_1}{T_1} = \frac{p_2 V_2}{T_2}$$

Assume that the balloon contains 100 cm³

$$\frac{98 \text{ kPa} \times 100 \text{ cm}^3}{287 \text{ K}} = \frac{1 \text{ kPa} \times V_2}{252 \text{ K}}$$

$$V_2 = 8605 \text{ cm}^3$$

$$\% \text{ increase} = 8605\%$$

(28)

The equation of state

$$pV = nRT \quad \text{is rearranged to} \quad R = \frac{pV}{nT}$$

$$n = \frac{m}{M} = \frac{0.27 \text{ g}}{32.0 \text{ g mol}^{-1}} = 8.4375 \times 10^{-3} \text{ mol}$$

The gas constant, $R = \dfrac{101.7 \times 10^3 \text{ Nm}^{-2} \times 1.9 \times 10^{-4} \text{ m}^3}{8.4375 \times 10^{-3} \text{ mol} \times 285 \text{ K}}$

$$= 8.036 \text{ JK}^{-1} \text{ mol}^{-1}$$

Correct answer, $R = 8.314 \text{ JK}^{-1} \text{ mol}^{-1}$

CHAPTER 6.
THERMOCHEMISTRY

(3)
(c)
(i)

Amount of carbon, $n = \dfrac{m}{M} = \dfrac{24.0\ \cancel{g}}{12.0\ \cancel{g}\ mol^{-1}} = 2.0\ mol\ C$

$$C(s) + \ O_2(g) = \ CO_2(g);\ \Delta H = -394\ kJ\ mol^{-1}$$
$$2C(s) + 2O_2(g) = 2CO_2(g);\ \Delta H = -394\ kJ\ \cancel{mol^{-1}} \times 2.0\ \cancel{mol}$$
$$= -788\ kJ$$

(ii)

$$3C(s) + 3O_2(g) = 3CO_2(g);\ \Delta H = -394\ kJ\ \cancel{mol^{-1}} \times 3\ \cancel{mol}$$
$$= -1182\ kJ$$

(iii)

$$0.25C(s) + 0.25O_2(g) = 0.25CO_2(g);\ \Delta H = -394\ kJ\ \cancel{mol^{-1}} \times 0.25\ \cancel{mol}$$
$$= -98.5\ kJ$$

(d)

$$C(s) + O_2(g) = CO_2(g);\ \Delta H = -394\ kJ\ mol^{-1}$$
$$M(C) = 12.0\ g\ mol^{-1}$$

394 kJ of energy are produced when 12.0 g of C is combusted.

98.5 kJ of energy are produced when $\dfrac{12.0\ g \times 98.5}{394} = 3\ g$ of C is combusted.

1970 kJ of energy are produced when $\dfrac{12.0\ g \times 1970}{394} = 60\ g$ of C is combusted.

(4)
(b)

$$\Delta H = mc_p\, \Delta T$$
$$130\ J = 0.015\ kg \times c_p \times 3.5\ K$$
$$c_p = 2476\ J\ kg^{-1}\ K^{-1}$$

(c)
Required:
$$CH_3COOH(l) + 2O_2(g) = 2CO_2(g) + 2H_2O(l); \Delta H = ?$$
Heat of combustion for 2.0 g of ethanoic acid

= heat absorbed by the calorimeter + heat absorbed by the water.

Heat absorbed by the calorimeter
$$\Delta H_1 = -mc_p \Delta T$$
$$= -2.8 \text{ kJ } °C^{-1} \times 5.95 °C$$
$$= -16.66 \text{ kJ}$$

Heat absorbed by the water
$$\Delta H_2 = -mc_p \Delta T$$
$$= -0.5 \text{ kg} \times 4.18 \text{ kJ kg}^{-1} °C^{-1} \times 5.95 °C$$
$$= -12.4355 \text{ kJ}$$

Heat of combustion for 2.0 g of ethanoic acid
$$= \Delta H_1 + \Delta H_2 = -16.66 \text{ kJ} - 12.4355 \text{ kJ}$$
$$= -29.0955 \text{ kJ}$$

This means that 29.0955 kJ of heat is released when 2.0 g of ethanoic acid is burnt in excess oxygen.
$$M(CH_3COOH) = 60 \text{ g mol}^{-1}$$

Amount of CH_3COOH, $n = \dfrac{m}{M} = \dfrac{0.2 \text{ g}}{60 \text{ g mol}^{-1}} = 0.0333$ mol

The standard molar heat of combustion of ethanoic acid
$$= \frac{-29.0955 \text{ kJ}}{0.0333 \text{ mol}} = -8729 \text{ kJ mol}^{-1}$$

(5)
Required:
$$CH_3COCH_3(l) + 4O_2(g) = 3CO_2(g) + 3H_2O(l); \Delta H = ?$$
Heat of combustion for 2.32 g of propanone

= heat absorbed by the water (calorimeter has a negligible heat capacity).

Heat absorbed by the water
$$\Delta H = -mc_p \Delta T$$
$$= -0.5 \text{ kg} \times 4.18 \text{ kJ kg}^{-1} °C^{-1} \times 25.5 °C$$
$$= -53.295 \text{ kJ}$$

This means that 53.295 kJ of heat is released when 2.32 g of propanone is burnt in excess oxygen.
$$M(CH_3COCH_3) = 58 \text{ g mol}^{-1}$$

Amount of CH_3COCH_3, $n = \dfrac{m}{M} = \dfrac{2.32 \text{ g}}{58 \text{ g mol}^{-1}} = 0.04$ mol

The standard molar heat of combustion of propanone

$$= \frac{-53.295 \text{ kJ}}{0.04 \text{ mol}} = -1332 \text{ kJ mol}^{-1}$$

(6)

$$C_7H_{16} + 11O_2 \rightarrow 7CO_2 + 8H_2O$$

(a)

1 g C_7H_{18} produces 48.5 kJ of energy

1000 g C_7H_{16} produces 48500 kJ of energy

The kilogram calorific value of heptane = 48500 kJ kg^{-1}

(b)

$$M(C_7H_{16}) = 100 \text{ g mol}^{-1}$$

1 g C_7H_{16} produces 48.5 kJ of energy

100 g C_7H_{16} produces 4850 kJ of energy

The molar heat of combustion of heptane = 4850 kJ mol^{-1}

(7)
(a)

$$CH_3OH + \tfrac{3}{2}O_2 \rightarrow CO_2 + 2H_2O; \Delta H = -\ 730 \text{ kJ mol}^{-1}$$
$$C_2H_5OH + 3O_2 \rightarrow 2CO_2 + 3H_2O; \Delta H = -1370 \text{ kJ mol}^{-1}$$
$$C_3H_7OH + \tfrac{9}{2}O_2 \rightarrow 3CO_2 + 4H_2O; \Delta H = -2020 \text{ kJ mol}^{-1}$$
$$C_4H_9OH + 6O_2 \rightarrow 4CO_2 + 5H_2O; \Delta H = -2650 \text{ kJ mol}^{-1}$$

(b)

$$M(CH_3OH) = 32 \text{ g mol}^{-1}$$

32 g $CH_3OH \rightarrow 730$ kJ energy

1000 g $CH_3OH \rightarrow \dfrac{730 \text{ kJ} \times 1000}{32} = 22813$ kJ energy

The kilogram calorific value of methanol = 22813 kJ kg^{-1}

$$M(C_2H_5OH) = 46 \text{ g mol}^{-1}$$

46 g $C_2H_5OH \rightarrow 730$ kJ energy

1000 g $C_2H_5OH \rightarrow \dfrac{1370 \text{ kJ} \times 1000}{46} = 29783$ kJ energy

The kilogram calorific value of ethanol = 29783 kJ kg^{-1}

$$M(C_3H_7OH) = 60 \text{ g mol}^{-1}$$

46 g $C_3H_7OH \rightarrow 2020$ kJ energy

1000 g $C_3H_7OH \rightarrow \dfrac{2020 \text{ kJ} \times 1000}{60} = 33667$ kJ energy

The kilogram calorific value of propanol = 33667 kJ kg^{-1}

$$M(C_4H_9OH) = 74 \text{ g mol}^{-1}$$

$$74 \text{ g } C_4H_9OH \rightarrow 2650 \text{ kJ energy}$$

$$1000 \text{ g } C_4H_9OH \rightarrow \frac{2650 \text{ kJ} \times 1000}{74} = 35811 \text{ kJ energy}$$

The kilogram calorific value of butanol = 35811 kJ kg^{-1}

(c)

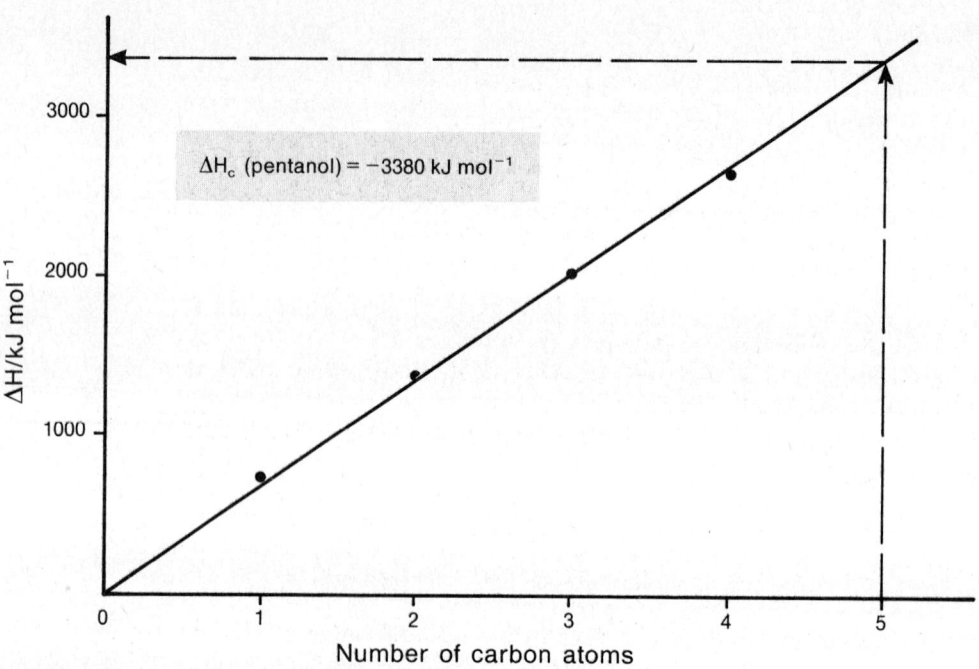

ΔH_c (pentanol) = $-3380 \text{ kJ mol}^{-1}$

(d)
Molar heat of combustion of pentanol = 3250 kJ mol^{-1}

(8)
Required:

$$2H_2S(g) + 3O_2(g) = 2H_2O(l) + 2SO_2(g); \Delta H = ?$$

[1] $H_2(g) + S(s) \quad = H_2S(g); \Delta H = -21 \text{ kJ mol}^{-1}$

[2] $H_2(g) + \frac{1}{2}O_2(g) = H_2O(l); \Delta H = -286 \text{ kJ mol}^{-1}$

[3] $S(s) + O_2(g) \quad = SO_2(g); \Delta H = -297 \text{ kJ mol}^{-1}$

30

$[3] \times 2 - [1] \times 2$

$$2S(s) + 2O_2(g) \quad = 2SO_2(g); \Delta H = -594 \text{ kJ mol}^{-1}$$

$$2H_2(g) + 2S(s) \quad = 2H_2S(s); \Delta H = -\ 42 \text{ kJ mol}^{-1}$$

$$2H_2S(g) + 2O_2(g) \quad = 2H_2(g) + 2SO_2(g); \Delta H = -552 \text{ kJ mol}^{-1} \ [4]$$

$[4] + [2] \times 2$

$$2H_2S(g) + 2O_2(g) \quad = 2H_2(g) + 2SO_2(g); \Delta H = -552 \text{ kJ mol}^{-1}$$

$$2H_2(g) + \ O_2(g) \quad = 2H_2O(l); \qquad \Delta H = -572 \text{ kJ mol}^{-1}$$

$$2H_2S(g) + 3O_2(g) \quad = 2H_2O(l) + 2SO_2(g); \Delta H = -1124 \text{ kJ mol}^{-1}$$

(10)

Required:

$$2H_2S(g) + SO_2(g) = 3S(s) + 2H_2O(l); \Delta H = ?$$

$[1] \quad H_2(g) + S(s) \qquad = H_2S(g); \Delta H = -\ 21 \text{ kJ mol}^{-1}$

$[2] \quad S(s) + O_2(g) \qquad = SO_2(g); \Delta H = -297 \text{ kJ mol}^{-1}$

$[3] \quad H_2(g) + \frac{1}{2}O_2(g) \quad = H_2O(l); \Delta H = -286 \text{ kJ mol}^{-1}$

$[3] - [1]$

$$H_2(g) + \tfrac{1}{2}O_2(g) \qquad = H_2O(l); \Delta H = -286 \text{ kJ mol}^{-1}$$

$$H_2(g) + S(s) \qquad = H_2S(g): \Delta H = -\ 21 \text{ kJ mol}^{-1}$$

$$H_2S(g) + \tfrac{1}{2}O_2(g) = H_2O(l) + S(s); \qquad \Delta H = -265 \text{ kJ mol}^{-1} \ [4]$$

$[4] \times 2 - [2]$

$$2H_2S(g) + O_2(g) \ = 2H_2O(l) + 2S(s); \quad \Delta H = -530 \text{ kJ mol}^{-1}$$

$$S(s) + O_2(g) \qquad = SO_2(g); \qquad \Delta H = -297 \text{ kJ mol}^{-1}$$

$$2H_2S(g) + SO_2(g) \ = 3S(s) + 2H_2O(l); \Delta H = -233 \text{ kJ mol}^{-1}$$

(11)

Required:

$$2C(s) + 3H_2(g) + \tfrac{1}{2}O_2(g) = C_2H_5OH(l); \Delta H = ?$$

$[1] \quad C(s) + O_2(g) \qquad\qquad = CO_2(g); \qquad \Delta H = -\ 394 \text{ kJ mol}^{-1}$

$[2] \quad H_2(g) + \tfrac{1}{2}O_2(g) \qquad = H_2O(l); \qquad \Delta H = -\ 286 \text{ kJ mol}^{-1}$

$[3] \quad C_2H_5OH(l) + 3O_2(g) = 2CO_2(g) + 3H_2O(l); \Delta H = -1370 \text{ kJ mol}^{-1}$

$[1] \times 2 - [3]$

$$2C(s) + 2O_2(g) \qquad\qquad = 2CO_2(g); \qquad \Delta H = -\ 788 \text{ kJ mol}^{-1}$$

$$C_2H_5OH(l) + 3O_2(g) \qquad = 2CO_2(g) + 3H_2O(l); \Delta H = -1370 \text{ kJ mol}^{-1}$$

$$2C(s) + 3H_2O(l) \qquad\qquad = C_2H_5OH(l) + O_2(g); \Delta H = +582 \text{ kJ mol}^{-1} \ [4]$$

31

$[4] + [2] \times 3$

$2C(s) + 3H_2O(l)$	$= C_2H_5OH(l) + O_2(g); \Delta H = +582 \text{ kJ mol}^{-1}$	
$3H_2(g) + \frac{3}{2}O_2(g)$	$= 3H_2O(l);$	$\Delta H = -858 \text{ kJ mol}^{-1}$

$2C(s) + 3H_2(g) + \frac{1}{2}O_2(g) \quad = C_2H_5OH(l); \qquad \Delta H = -276 \text{ kJ mol}^{-1}$

(12)
Required:

$$C_2H_5OH(l) + 3O_2(g) = 2CO_2(g) + 2H_2O(l); \Delta H = ?$$

Heat of combustion for 0.92 g of ethanol

= heat absorbed by the calorimeter, the calorimeter fittings and the water

Heat absorbed

$$\Delta H = -mc_p \Delta T$$

$$= -3.6 \text{ kJ } °C^{-1} \times 7.5 °C$$

$$= -27.0 \text{ kJ}$$

$$M(C_2H_5OH) = 46 \text{ g mol}^{-1}$$

Amount of CH_3COOH, $n = \dfrac{m}{M} = \dfrac{0.92 \text{ g}}{46 \text{ g mol}^{-1}} = 0.02 \text{ mol}$

The standard molar heat of combustion of ethanol

$$= \frac{-27.0 \text{ kJ}}{0.02 \text{ mol}} = -1350 \text{ kJ mol}^{-1}$$

This value compares very favourably with the value quoted $(-1370 \text{ kJ mol}^{-1})$ in question 11. The value differs due to the usual experimental errors.

(13)

$$HNO_3(aq) + NaOH(aq) \rightarrow NaNO_3(aq) + H_2O(l)$$

Assume that the densities of dilute acid and dilute base are equal to the density of water (1 g/cm^3) and that their specific heat capacities are equal to the specific heat capacity of water.

Heat Change $= -mc_p \Delta T$

$$= -0.5 \text{ kg} \times 4.2 \text{ kJ kg}^{-1} °C^{-1} \times 1.35 °C$$

$$= -2.835 \text{ kJ}$$

The amounts used, $n = cV$

The amount of NaOH, $n = 0.2 \text{ mol dm}^{-3} \times 0.25 \text{ dm}^3 \text{ NaOH}$

$$= 0.05 \text{ mol NaOH}$$

The amount of HNO_3, $n = 0.2$ mol dm^{-3} × 0.25 dm^3 HCl

$$= 0.05 \text{ mol } HNO_3$$

Because the standard heat of neutralisation refers to one mole of H^+ ions reacting with one mole of OH^- ions, then

$$\Delta H = \frac{-2.835 \text{ kJ}}{0.05 \text{ mol}} = -56.7 \text{ kJ mol}^{-1}$$

(14)

Amount of Ca, $n = \dfrac{m}{M} = \dfrac{0.8 \text{ g}}{40 \text{ g mol}^{-1}} = 0.02$ mol Ca

Amount of HNO_3, $n = cV = 1.0$ mol dm^{-3} × 0.2 dm^3 HCl

$$= 0.02 \text{ mol } HNO_3$$

$$Ca(s) + 2HNO_3(aq) \rightarrow Ca(NO_3)_2(aq) + H_2(g)$$

1 mol Ca reacts with 2 mol HNO_3

0.02 mol Ca reacts with 0.04 mol HNO_3

As $0.2 > 0.04$, then calcium is the limiting reactant.

$$\text{Heat Change} = -mc_p \, \Delta T$$

$$= -0.2 \text{ kg} \times 4.2 \text{ kJ kg}^{-1} \, {}^\circ C^{-1} \times 6.0 \, {}^\circ C$$

$$= -5.04 \text{ kJ}$$

The molar heat of reaction (for one mol of Ca)

$$\Delta H = \frac{-5.04 \text{ kJ}}{0.02 \text{ mol}} = -252 \text{ kJ mol}^{-1}$$

(15)

Amount of NH_4Cl, $n = \dfrac{m}{M} = \dfrac{10.7 \text{ g}}{53.5 \text{ g mol}^{-1}} = 0.2$ mol NH_4Cl

$$\text{Heat Change} = -mc_p \, \Delta T$$

$$= -0.5 \text{ kg} \times 4.2 \text{ kJ kg}^{-1} \, {}^\circ C^{-1} \times (-1.6 \, {}^\circ C)$$

$$= +3.36 \text{ kJ}$$

The heat of solution for 1 mol NH_4Cl

$$\Delta H = \frac{+3.36 \text{ kJ}}{0.2 \text{ mol}} = +16.8 \text{ kJ mol}^{-1}$$

(16)

Amount of Mg, $n = \dfrac{m}{M} = \dfrac{0.72\,g}{24.0\,g\,mol^{-1}} = 0.03$ mol NH_4Cl

Amount of HCl, $n = cV = 1.0$ mol $dm^{-3} \times 0.3$ dm^3 HCl

$$= 0.3 \text{ mol HCl}$$

$$Mg(s) + 2HCl(aq) \rightarrow MgCl_2(aq) + H_2(g)$$

1 mol Mg reacts with 2 mol HCl

0.03 mol Mg reacts with 0.06 mol HCl

As $0.3 > 0.06$, HCl is in excess and magnesium is the limiting reactant.

$$\text{Heat change} = -mc_p\,\Delta T$$

$$= -0.3\,kg \times 4.2\,kJ\,kg^{-1}\,{}^\circ C^{-1} \times 10.1\,{}^\circ C$$

$$= -12.726 \text{ kJ}$$

Molar heat of reaction

$$\Delta H = \frac{-12.726\text{ kJ}}{0.03\text{ mol}} = -424.2\,kJ\,mol^{-1}$$

(17)

$$H-H + Cl-Cl \rightarrow 2H-Cl$$

$\Delta H =$ Sum of the Energy of the Bonds Broken
      $-$ Sum of the Energy of the Bonds Formed

$$\Delta H = +E(H-H) + E(Cl-Cl) - 2E(H-Cl)$$

$$= (+436 + 339 - 2 \times 431)\,kJ\,mol^{-1}$$

$$= -87\,kJ\,mol^{-1}$$

(18)
(i)

$$N_2(g) + 3H_2(g) = 2NH_3(g); \Delta H = ?$$

$$N\equiv N + 3H-H = 2 \quad \overset{\displaystyle H}{\underset{\displaystyle H}{\overset{|}{\underset{|}{N-H}}}}; \Delta H = ?$$

$\Delta H =$ Sum of the Energy of the Bonds Broken
$\quad$ – Sum of the Energy of the Bonds Formed

$$\Delta H = + E(N\equiv N) + 3E(H-H) - 2 \times 3E(N-H)$$
$$= (+941 + 3 \times 436 - 6 \times 391) \text{ kJ mol}^{-1}$$
$$= -97 \text{ kJ mol}^{-1}$$

(ii)

$$C_3H_6(g) + H_2(g) = C_3H_8(g)$$

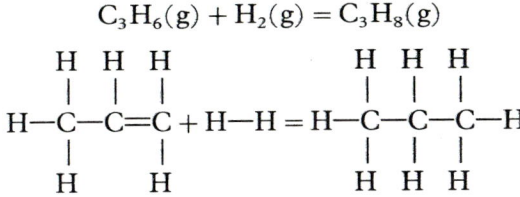

$\Delta H =$ Sum of the Energy of the Bonds Broken
$\quad$ – Sum of the Energy of the Bonds Formed

$$\Delta H = + 6E(C-H) + E(C-C) + E(C=C) + E(H-H)$$
$$- 8E(C-H) - 2E(C-C)$$
$$= - 2E(C-H) - E(C-C) + E(C=C) + E(H-H)$$
$$= (-2 \times 413 - 348 + 619 + 436) \text{ kJ mol}^{-1}$$
$$= - 119 \text{ kJ mol}^{-1}$$

(19)

$$2H_2(g) + O_2(g) = 2H_2O(g); \Delta H = ?$$

$$2H-H + O=O \rightarrow 2H-O-H$$

$\Delta H =$ Sum of the Energy of the Bonds Broken
$\quad$ – Sum of the Energy of the Bonds Formed

$$\Delta H = + 2E(H-H) + E(O=O) - 2E(H-O)$$
$$= (+2 \times 436 + 497 - 2 \times 463) \text{ kJ mol}^{-1}$$
$$= + 443 \text{ kJ mol}^{-1}$$

(20)

$$C(\text{graphite}) + 2H_2(g) + \tfrac{1}{2}O_2(g) = CH_3OH(g); \Delta H = ?$$

$$
\begin{array}{c}
\phantom{C(\text{graphite}) + 2H-H + \tfrac{1}{2}O=O = H-} H \\
\phantom{C(\text{graphite}) + 2H-H + \tfrac{1}{2}O=O = H-} | \\
C(\text{graphite}) + 2H{-}H + \tfrac{1}{2}O{=}O = H{-}C{-}O{-}H \\
\phantom{C(\text{graphite}) + 2H-H + \tfrac{1}{2}O=O = H-} | \\
\phantom{C(\text{graphite}) + 2H-H + \tfrac{1}{2}O=O = H-} H
\end{array}
$$

$\Delta H =$ Sum of the Energy of the Bonds Broken
 $-$ Sum of the Energy of the Bonds Formed

$$
\begin{aligned}
\Delta H ={}& +E(C(\text{graphite}) \rightarrow C(g)) + 2E(H{-}H) + \tfrac{1}{2}E(O{=}O) \\
& - 3E(C{-}H) - E(C{-}O) - E(O{-}H) \\
={}& (+717 + 2 \times 436 + \tfrac{1}{2} \times 497 - 3 \times 413 - 360 - 463)\ \text{kJ mol}^{-1} \\
={}& -224.5\ \text{kJ mol}^{-1}
\end{aligned}
$$

(21)

$$CH_3OH(g) + HCl(g) = CH_3Cl(g) + H_2O(g); \Delta H = ?$$

$$
\begin{array}{ccccc}
H & & H & & \\
| & & | & & \\
H{-}C{-}O{-}H + H{-}Cl & = & H{-}C{-}Cl + H{-}O & & \\
| & & | & & \backslash \\
H & & H & & H
\end{array}
$$

$\Delta H =$ Sum of the Energy of the Bonds Broken
 $-$ Sum of the Energy of the Bonds Formed

$$
\begin{aligned}
\Delta H ={}& +3E(C{-}H) + E(C{-}O) + E(O{-}H) + E(H{-}Cl) \\
& - 3E(C{-}H) - E(C{-}Cl) - 2E(O{-}H) \\
={}& +E(C{-}O) + E(H{-}Cl) - E(C{-}Cl) - E(O{-}H) \\
={}& (+360 + 431 - 328 - 463)\ \text{kJ mol}^{-1} \\
={}& 0
\end{aligned}
$$

(22)
(iii)

Amount of C_2H_5OH, $n = \dfrac{m}{M} = \dfrac{0.9\ \cancel{g}}{46.0\ \cancel{g}\ \text{mol}^{-1}} = 0.0196\ \text{mol}\ C_2H_5OH$

(iv)

$$
\begin{aligned}
\text{Heat Change} &= -mc_p\,\Delta T \\
&= -0.5\ \cancel{kg} \times 4.2\ \text{kJ}\ \cancel{kg}^{-1}\ \cancel{{}^\circ C}^{-1} \times 10.1\ \cancel{{}^\circ C} \\
&= -21.21\ \text{kJ}
\end{aligned}
$$

(v)
Molar heat of reaction

$$\Delta H = \frac{-21.21\ \text{kJ}}{0.0196\ \text{mol}} = -1084\ \text{kJ mol}^{-1}$$

(23)

(a)

$$HCl(aq) + NaOH(aq) \rightarrow NaCl(aq) + H_2O(l)$$

$$\text{Heat Change} = -mc_p\,\Delta T$$

$$= -0.1\,\cancel{kg} \times 4.2\,kJ\,\cancel{kg^{-1}}\,\cancel{°C^{-1}} \times 6.85\,\cancel{°C}$$

$$= -2.877\,kJ$$

The amounts used, $n = cV$

The amount of NaOH, $n = 1.0\,mol\,\cancel{dm^{-3}} \times 0.05\,\cancel{dm^3}\,NaOH$

$$= 0.05\,mol\,NaOH$$

The amount of HCl, $n = 1.0\,mol\,\cancel{dm^{-3}} \times 0.05\,\cancel{dm^3}\,HCl$

$$= 0.05\,mol\,HCl$$

Because the standard heat of neutralisation refers to one mole of H^+ ions reacting with one mole of OH^-, then

$$\Delta H = \frac{-2.877\,kJ}{0.05\,mol} = -57.54\,kJ\,mol^{-1}$$

(b)

$$HCOOH(aq) + NaOH(aq) \rightarrow NaCl(aq) + H_2O(l)$$

$$\text{Heat Change} = -mc_p\,\Delta T$$

$$= -0.1\,\cancel{kg} \times 4.2\,kJ\,\cancel{kg^{-1}}\,\cancel{°C^{-1}} \times 5.3\,\cancel{°C}$$

$$= -2.226\,kJ$$

The amount used, $n = cV$

The amount of NaOH, $n = 1.0\,mol\,\cancel{dm^{-3}} \times 0.05\,\cancel{dm^3}\,NaOH$

$$= 0.05\,mol\,NaOH$$

The amount of HCOOH, $n = 1.0\,mol\,\cancel{dm^{-3}} \times 0.05\,\cancel{dm^3}\,HCOOH$

$$0.05\,mol\,HCOOH$$

Because the standard heat of neutralisation refers to one mole of H^+ ions reacting with one mole of OH^- ions, then

$$\Delta H = \frac{-2.226\,kJ}{0.05\,mol} = -44.52\,kJ\,mol^{-1}$$

Heat of ionisation of methanoic acid $= (57.54 - 44.52)\,kJ\,mol^{-1}$
$$= 13.02\,kJ\,mol^{-1}$$

(24)

$$C_6H_{14}(g) \rightarrow 6C(g) + 14H(g); \Delta H = +7512 \text{ kJ mol}^{-1}$$
$$C_7H_{16}(g) \rightarrow 7C(g) + 16H(g); \Delta H = +8684 \text{ kJ mol}^{-1}$$

$$
\begin{array}{cccccc}
H & H & H & H & H & H \\
| & | & | & | & | & | \\
H-C-&C-&C-&C-&C-&C-H \rightarrow 6C(g) + 14H(g); \Delta H = +7512 \text{ kJ mol}^{-1}\\
| & | & | & | & | & | \\
H & H & H & H & H & H
\end{array}
$$

$$
\begin{array}{ccccccc}
H & H & H & H & H & H & H \\
| & | & | & | & | & | & | \\
H-C-&C-&C-&C-&C-&C-&C-H \rightarrow 7C(g) + 16H(g); \Delta H = +8684 \text{ kJ mol}^{-1}\\
| & | & | & | & | & | & | \\
H & H & H & H & H & H & H
\end{array}
$$

[1] $5E(C-C) + 14E(C-H) = 7512 \text{ kJ mol}^{-1}$

[2] $6E(C-C) + 16E(C-H) = 8684 \text{ kJ mol}^{-1}$

$[1] \times 6 - [2] \times 5$

$$
\begin{aligned}
30E(C-C) + 84E(C-H) &= 45072 \text{ kJ mol}^{-1}\\
30E(C-C) + 80E(C-H) &= 43420 \text{ kJ mol}^{-1}\\
\hline
4E(C-H) &= 1652 \text{ kJ mol}^{-1}\\
E(C-H) &= 413 \text{ kJ mol}^{-1}
\end{aligned}
$$

Substituting the value for $E(C-H)$ into [1]

$$
\begin{aligned}
5E(C-C) + 14 \times 413 \text{ kJ mol}^{-1} &= 7512 \text{ kJ mol}^{-1}\\
5E(C-C) &= 1730 \text{ kJ mol}^{-1}\\
E(C-C) &= 346 \text{ kJ mol}^{-1}
\end{aligned}
$$

(25)
(a)
Required:

$$2C(s) + 2H_2(g) = C_2H_4(g); \Delta H = ?$$

[1] $H_2(g) + \frac{1}{2}O_2(g) = H_2O(l); \Delta H = -286 \text{ kJ mol}^{-1}$

[2] $C(s) + O_2(g) \quad = CO_2(g); \Delta H = -394 \text{ kJ mol}^{-1}$

[3] $C_2H_4(g) + 3O_2(g) = 2CO_2(g) + 2H_2O(l); \Delta H = -1411 \text{ kJ mol}^{-1}$

$[3] - [2] \times 2$

$C_2H_4(g) + 3O_2(g) = 2CO_2(g) + 2H_2O(l); \Delta H = -1411 \text{ kJ mol}^{-1}$

$2C(s) + 2O_2(g) \quad = 2CO_2(g); \Delta H = -788 \text{ kJ mol}^{-1}$

$C_2H_4(g) + O_2(g) \quad = 2C(s) + 2H_2O(l); \Delta H = -623 \text{ kJ mol}^{-1}$ [4]

$[4] - [2] \times 2$

$C_2H_4(g) + O_2(g) = 2C(s) + 2H_2O(l); \Delta H = -623 \text{ kJ mol}^{-1}$ [4]

$2H_2(g) + O_2(g) \quad = 2H_2O(l); \Delta H = -572 \text{ kJ mol}^{-1}$

$2C(s) + 2H_2(g) \quad = C_2H_4(g); \Delta H = -51 \text{ kJ mol}^{-1}$

Reversing

$$2C(s) + 2H_2(g) = C_2H_4(g); \Delta H = +51 \text{ kJ mol}^{-1}$$

(b)

$2C(s) + 2H_2(g) = C_2H_4(g): \Delta H = +51 \text{ kJ mol}^{-1}$

$$\begin{matrix} & & & \text{H} & \text{H} \\ & & & | & | \\ 2C(s) + 2H\text{—}H & = & H\text{—}C & \!\!=\!\! & C\text{—}H \end{matrix}$$

$\Delta H =$ Sum of the Energy of the Bonds Broken
$\quad -$ Sum of the Energy of the Bonds Formed

$\Delta H = +2E(C(s) \rightarrow C(g)) + 2E(H\text{—}H)$
$\quad - 4E(C\text{—}H) - E(C\text{=}C)$

$51 \text{ kJ mol}^{-1} = (2 \times 715 + 2 \times 436 - 4 \times 412 - E(C\text{=}C)) \text{ kJ mol}^{-1}$
$E(C\text{=}C) = 603 \text{ kJ mol}^{-1}$

(26)
(i)

$$C_6H_{14}(g) + \tfrac{19}{2}O_2(g) \rightarrow 6CO_2(g) + 7H_2O(g); \Delta H = ?$$

(ii)

$$M(C_6H_{14}) = 86.0 \text{ g mol}^{-1}$$

$$4.3 \text{ g } C_6H_{14} \rightarrow 210 \text{ kJ}$$

(a)

$$86.0 \text{ g } C_6H_{14} \rightarrow \frac{210 \times 86.0}{4.3} \text{ kJ} = 4200 \text{ kJ mol}^{-1}$$

(b)

$$1000 \text{ g } C_6H_{14} \rightarrow \frac{210 \times 1000}{4.3} \text{ kJ} = 48837 \text{ kJ kg}^{-1}$$

39

(iii)

Required: $6C(g) + 7H_2(g) \rightarrow C_6H_{14}(g); \Delta H = ?$

[1] $H_2(g) + \frac{1}{2}O_2(g) = H_2O(l); \Delta H = -286 \text{ kJ mol}^{-1}$

[2] $C(s) + O_2(g) = CO_2(g); \Delta H = -394 \text{ kJ mol}^{-1}$

[3] $C_6H_{14}(g) + \frac{19}{2}O_2(g) = 6CO_2(g) + 7H_2O(g); \Delta H = -4200 \text{ kJ mol}^{-1}$

[3] − [2] × 6

$C_6H_{14}(g) + \frac{19}{2}O_2(g) = 6CO_2(g) + 7H_2O(g): \Delta H = -4200 \text{ kJ mol}^{-1}$

$6C(s) + 6O_2(g) = 6CO_2(g): \Delta H = -2364 \text{ kJ mol}^{-1}$

―――

$C_6H_{14}(g) + \frac{7}{2}O_2(g) = 6C(s) + 7H_2O(g); \Delta H = -1836 \text{ kJ mol}^{-1}$ [4]

[4] − [1] × 7

$C_6H_{14}(g) + \frac{7}{2}O_2(g) = 6C(s) + 7H_2O(g); \Delta H = -1836 \text{ kJ mol}^{-1}$

$7H_2(g) + \frac{7}{2}O_2(g) = 7H_2O(1); \Delta H = -2002 \text{ kJ mol}^{-1}$

―――

$C_6H_{14}(g) = 6C(g) + 7H_2(g); \Delta H = +166 \text{ kJ mol}^{-1}$

Reversing

$$6C(g) + 7H_2(g) \rightarrow C_6H_{14}(g); \Delta H = -166 \text{ kJ mol}^{-1}$$

(iv)

$$6C(s) + 7H\text{—}H \rightarrow \begin{matrix} & H & H & H & H & H & H \\ & | & | & | & | & | & | \\ H\text{—} & C\text{—}C\text{—}C\text{—}C\text{—}C\text{—}C & \text{—}H \\ & | & | & | & | & | & | \\ & H & H & H & H & H & H \end{matrix}$$

$$6C(s) + 7H\text{—}H \rightarrow \begin{matrix} & H & H & H & H & H & H \\ & | & | & | & | & | & | \\ H\text{—} & C\text{—}C\text{—}C\text{—}C\text{—}C\text{—}C & \text{—}H \\ & | & | & | & | & | & | \\ & H & H & H & H & H & H \end{matrix}$$

ΔH = Sum of the Energy of the Bonds Broken
− Sum of the Energy of the Bonds Formed

$$\Delta H = +6E(C(s) \rightarrow C(g)) + 7E(H\text{—}H)$$
$$- 14E(C\text{—}H) - 5E(C\text{—}C)$$

$-166 \text{ kJ mol}^{-1} = (6 \times 715 + 7 \times 436 - 14 \times 412 - 5E(C\text{—}C)) \text{ kJ mol}^{-1}$
$5E(C{=}C) = 1740 \text{ kJ mol}^{-1}$
$E(C{=}C) = 348 \text{ kJ mol}^{-1}$

$$6C(s) + 3H_2(g) = C_6H_6(g); \Delta H = +83 \text{ kJ mol}^{-1}$$

$$6C(s) + 3H{-}H \rightarrow$$

$\Delta H = $ Sum of the Energy of the Bonds Broken
$\quad$ $-$ Sum of the Energy of the Bonds Formed

$\Delta H = +6E(C(s) \rightarrow C(g)) + 3E(H{-}H)$
$\quad -6E(C{-}H) - 3E(C{=}C) - 3E(C{-}C)$

$\Delta H = (6 \times 715 + 3 \times 436 - 6 \times 412 - 3 \times 619 - 3 \times 348) \text{ kJ mol}^{-1}$
$\quad = +225 \text{ kJ mol}^{-1}$

CHAPTER 7.
RATES OF CHEMICAL
REACTIONS

7(5)

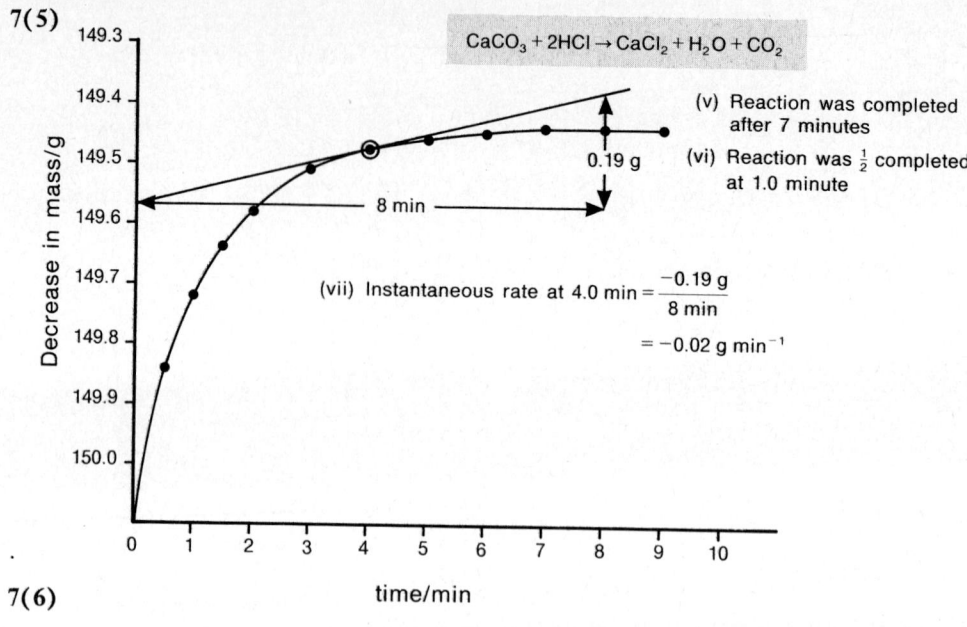

$$CaCO_3 + 2HCl \rightarrow CaCl_2 + H_2O + CO_2$$

(v) Reaction was completed after 7 minutes

(vi) Reaction was $\frac{1}{2}$ completed at 1.0 minute

0.19 g

8 min

(vii) Instantaneous rate at 4.0 min $= \dfrac{-0.19 \text{ g}}{8 \text{ min}}$

$= -0.02 \text{ g min}^{-1}$

Decrease in mass/g

time/min

7(6)

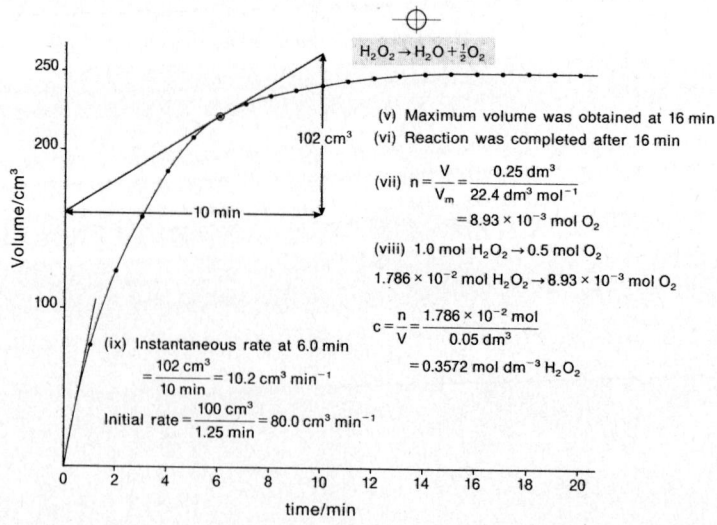

$$H_2O_2 \rightarrow H_2O + \tfrac{1}{2}O_2$$

(v) Maximum volume was obtained at 16 min

(vi) Reaction was completed after 16 min

(vii) $n = \dfrac{V}{V_m} = \dfrac{0.25 \text{ dm}^3}{22.4 \text{ dm}^3 \text{ mol}^{-1}}$

$= 8.93 \times 10^{-3} \text{ mol O}_2$

(viii) 1.0 mol $H_2O_2 \rightarrow 0.5$ mol O_2

1.786×10^{-2} mol $H_2O_2 \rightarrow 8.93 \times 10^{-3}$ mol O_2

$c = \dfrac{n}{V} = \dfrac{1.786 \times 10^{-2} \text{ mol}}{0.05 \text{ dm}^3}$

$= 0.3572 \text{ mol dm}^{-3} \text{ H}_2\text{O}_2$

102 cm³

10 min

(ix) Instantaneous rate at 6.0 min

$= \dfrac{102 \text{ cm}^3}{10 \text{ min}} = 10.2 \text{ cm}^3 \text{ min}^{-1}$

Initial rate $= \dfrac{100 \text{ cm}^3}{1.25 \text{ min}} = 80.0 \text{ cm}^3 \text{ min}^{-1}$

Volume/cm³

time/min

7(13)

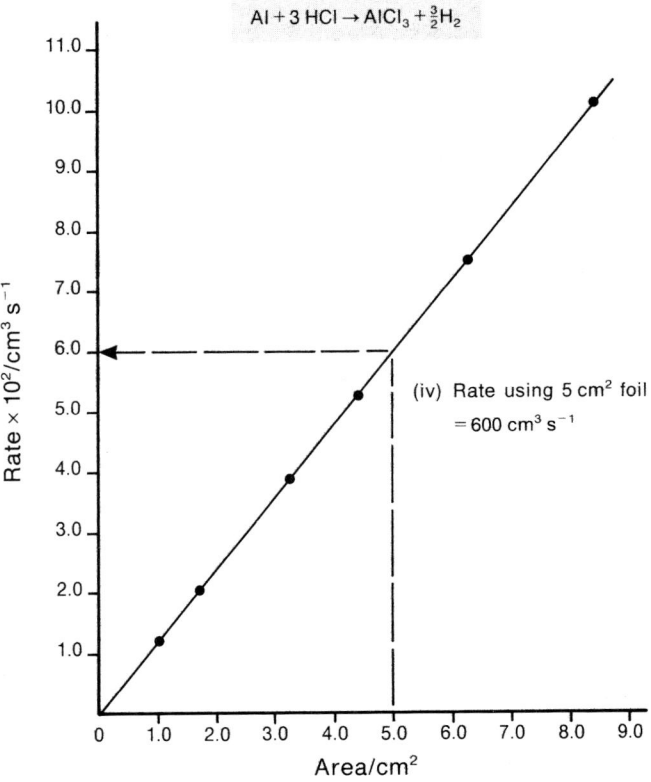

$$Al + 3\,HCl \rightarrow AlCl_3 + \tfrac{3}{2}H_2$$

(iv) Rate using 5 cm² foil
= 600 cm³ s⁻¹

Rate × 10²/cm³ s⁻¹

Area/cm²

7(14)

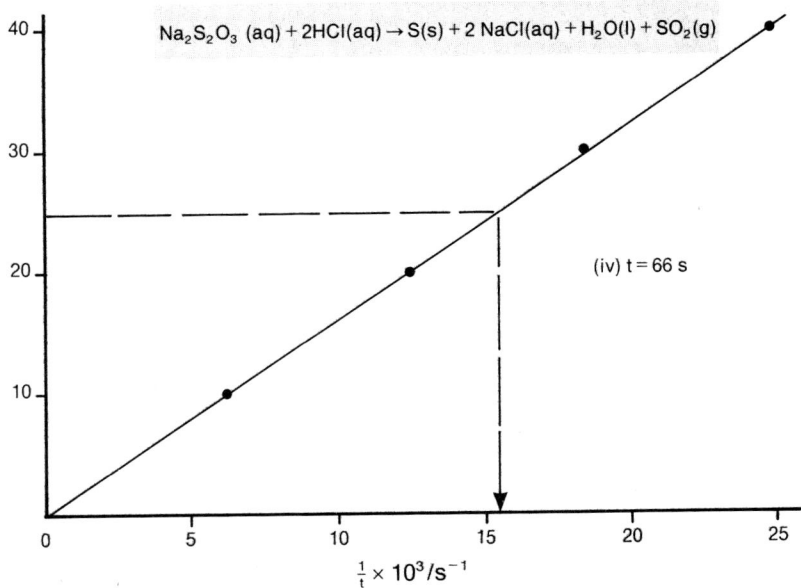

$$Na_2S_2O_3\,(aq) + 2HCl(aq) \rightarrow S(s) + 2\,NaCl(aq) + H_2O(l) + SO_2(g)$$

(iv) t = 66 s

$\frac{1}{t} \times 10^3/s^{-1}$

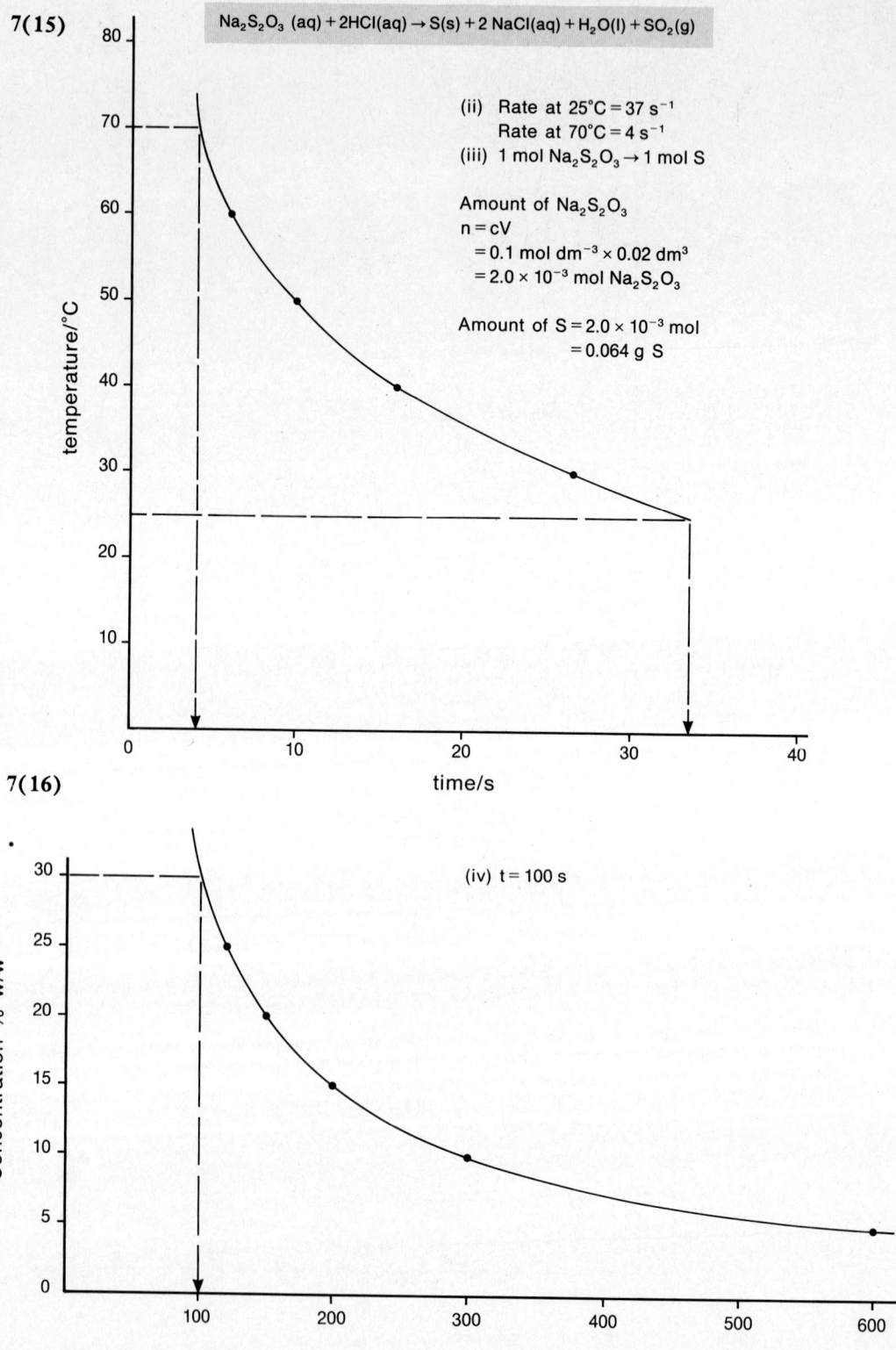

7(15)

$Na_2S_2O_3 \ (aq) + 2HCl(aq) \rightarrow S(s) + 2 \ NaCl(aq) + H_2O(l) + SO_2(g)$

(ii) Rate at 25°C = 37 s^{-1}
     Rate at 70°C = 4 s^{-1}
(iii) 1 mol $Na_2S_2O_3 \rightarrow$ 1 mol S

Amount of $Na_2S_2O_3$
n = cV
  = 0.1 mol dm^{-3} × 0.02 dm^3
  = 2.0 × 10^{-3} mol $Na_2S_2O_3$

Amount of S = 2.0 × 10^{-3} mol
           = 0.064 g S

temperature/°C

time/s

7(16)

(iv) t = 100 s

Concentration % w/w

time/s

CHAPTER 8. CHEMICAL EQUILIBRIUM

(1)

$$CH_3COOH(l) + C_2H_5OH(l) \rightleftharpoons CH_3COOC_2H_5(l) + H_2O(l)$$

Amount of CH_3COOH, $n = \dfrac{m}{M} = \dfrac{20.0 \text{ g}}{60 \text{ g mol}^{-1}} = 0.33 \text{ mol}$

Amount of $CH_3COOC_2H_5$, $n = \dfrac{m}{M} = \dfrac{58.0 \text{ g}}{74 \text{ g mol}^{-1}} = 0.66 \text{ mol}$

Amount of H_2O, $n = \dfrac{m}{M} = \dfrac{12.0 \text{ g}}{18 \text{ g mol}^{-1}} = 0.66 \text{ mol } CH_3COOH$

Let $x =$ amount of C_2H_5OH at equilibrium

$$K_c = \frac{[CH_3COOC_2H_5][H_2O]}{[CH_3COOH][C_2H_5OH]} = 4.0$$

$$4.0 = \frac{(0.66 \text{ mol})(0.66 \text{ mol})}{(0.33 \text{ mol}) \cdot x}$$

$$x = 0.33 \text{ mol}$$

Amount of C_2H_5OH at equilibrium $= 0.33 \text{ mol } C_2H_5OH$

(2)

$$SO_2Cl_2(g) \rightleftharpoons SO_2(g) + Cl_2(g)$$

$$K_c = \frac{[SO_2][Cl_2]}{[SO_2Cl_2]}$$

Amount of $SOCl_2$ at equilibrium, $n = \dfrac{m}{M} = \dfrac{13.5 \text{ g}}{135 \text{ g mol}^{-1}} = 0.1 \text{ mol}$

Concentration/mol dm^{-3}	SO_2Cl_2	SO_2	Cl_2
Initial	$\dfrac{0.1}{2}$	0	0
Change	$\dfrac{-x}{2}$	$\dfrac{+x}{2}$	$\dfrac{+x}{2}$
Equilibrium	$\dfrac{0.1-0.07}{2}$	$\dfrac{0.07}{2}$	$\dfrac{0.07}{2}$

$$K_c = \frac{[SO_2][Cl_2]}{[SO_2Cl_2]} = \frac{0.035 \text{ mol dm}^{-3} \times 0.035 \text{ mol dm}^{-3}}{0.015 \text{ mol dm}^{-3}}$$

$$= 0.0817 \text{ mol dm}^{-3}$$

(10)

$$N_2(g) + O_2(g) \rightleftharpoons 2NO(g); \; K_c = 2.5 \times 10^3 \text{ at } 2400 \text{ K}$$

Let x = molar change in concentration of each species

Concentration/mol dm^{-3}	N_2	O_2	NO
Change	$-x$	$-x$	$+2x$
Equilibrium	0.016	0.036	$+2x$

$$K_c = \frac{[NO]^2}{[N_2][O_2]} = 2.5 \times 10^3 \text{ at } 2400 \text{ K}$$

$$\frac{(2x)^2}{(0.016)(0.036)} = 2.5 \times 10^3 \text{ at } 2400 \text{ K}$$

$$x^2 = 0.36$$

$$x = 0.6, \; 2x = 1.2$$

Therefore, the equilibrium concentration of NO = 1.2 mol dm^{-3}

(11)

$$PCl_5(g) \rightleftharpoons PCl_3(g) + Cl_2(g)$$

Required: $K_c = \dfrac{[PCl_3][Cl_2]}{[PCl_5]} = ?$ at 433 K

Concentration/mol dm^{-3}	PCl$_5$	PCl$_3$	Cl$_2$
Initial	1.0	0	0
Change	$-x$	$+x$	$+x$
Equilibrium	0.865	0.135	0.135

$$K_c = \frac{[PCl_3][Cl_2]}{[PCl_5]} = \frac{0.135 \text{ mol dm}^{-3} \times 0.135 \text{ mol dm}^{-3}}{0.835 \text{ mol dm}^{-3}}$$

$$= 0.0218 \text{ mol dm}^{-3}$$

(12)

$$CO(g) + 2H_2(g) \rightleftharpoons CH_3OH(1)$$

$$K_c = \frac{[CH_3OH]}{[CO][H]^2} = ?$$

Concentration/mol dm^{-3}	CO	H$_2$	CH$_3$OH
Initial	0.1	0.2	0
Change	$-x$	$-2x$	$+x$
Equilibrium	0.0791	0.1582	0.0209

$$K_c = \frac{[CH_3OH]}{[CO][H_2]^2} = \frac{0.0209 \text{ mol dm}^{-3}}{0.0791 \text{ mol dm}^{-3} \times (0.1582 \text{ mol dm}^{-3})^2}$$

$$= 10.56 \text{ mol}^{-2} \text{ dm}^6$$

(13)

$$H_2(g) + I_2(g) \rightleftharpoons 2HI(g)$$

$$K_c = \frac{[HI]^2}{[H_2][I_2]} = 49.0 \text{ at } 717 \text{ K}$$

Let x = molar change in concentration of each species

Concentration/mol dm^{-3}	H$_2$	I$_2$	HI
Initial	3.00/5	2.00/5	0
Change	$-x$	$-x$	$+2x$
Equilibrium	$0.6 - x$	$0.4 - x$	$+2x$

$$K_c = \frac{[HI]^2}{[H_2][I_2]} = 49.0$$

$$\frac{(2x)^2}{(0.6 - x)(0.4 - x)} = 49.0$$

$$49.0 = \frac{4x^2}{0.24 - 1.0x + x^2}$$

Solving the quadratic equation,

$$x = 0.357 \text{ (or 0.732, which is not possible)}$$

The equilibrium concentrations are as follows

$$[H_2] = (0.6 - 0.357) \text{ mol dm}^{-3} = 0.243 \text{ mol dm}^{-3}$$
$$[I_2] = (0.4 - 0.357) \text{ mol dm}^{-3} = 0.043 \text{ mol dm}^{-3}$$
$$[HI] = 2 \times 0.357 \text{ mol dm}^{-3} = 0.714 \text{ mol dm}^{-3}$$

(14)

$$Br_2(g) + Cl_2(g) \rightleftharpoons 2BrCl(g): K_c = 7.0 \text{ at } 125\,°C$$

Let x = molar change in concentration of each species

Concentration/mol dm^{-3}	Br$_2$	Cl$_2$	BrCl
Initial	0.6/10	0.6/10	0
Change	$-x$	$-x$	$+2x$
Equilibrium	$0.06 - x$	$0.06 - x$	$+2x$

$$K_c = \frac{[BrCl]^2}{[Br_2][Cl_2]} = 7.0$$

$$\frac{(2x)^2}{(0.06 - x)(0.06 - x)} = 7.0$$

$$7.0 = \frac{4x^2}{0.0036 - 0.12x + x^2}$$

Solving the quadratic equation,

$$x = 0.034 \text{ (or 0.246, which is not possible)}$$

The equilibrium concentrations are as follows

$$[Br_2] = (0.06 - 0.034) \text{ mol dm}^{-3} = 0.026 \text{ mol dm}^{-3}$$
$$[Cl_2] = (0.06 - 0.034) \text{ mol dm}^{-3} = 0.026 \text{ mol dm}^{-3}$$
$$[BrCl] = 2 \times 0.034 \text{ mol dm}^{-3} = 0.068 \text{ mol dm}^{-3}$$

(16)

$$2HI(g) \rightleftharpoons H_2(g) + I_2(g)$$

$$K_c = \frac{[H_2][I_2]}{[HI]^2} = ? \text{ at } 670 \text{ K}$$

Let $1.0 = $ initial molar concentration of HI

Concentration/mol dm^{-3}	HI	H$_2$	I$_2$
Initial	1.0	0	0
Change	0.2	0.1	0.1
Equilibrium	0.8	0.1	0.1

$$K_c = \frac{[H_2][I_2]}{[HI]^2} = \frac{0.1 \text{ mol dm}^{-3} \times 0.1 \text{ mol dm}^{-3}}{(0.8 \text{ mol dm}^{-3})^2}$$

$$= 1.5625 \times 10^{-3}$$

(17)

$$COCl_2(g) \rightleftharpoons CO(g) + Cl_2(g)$$

$$K_c = \frac{[CO][Cl_2]}{[COCl_2]} = ?$$

$x = $ change in molar concentration of each species $= 16\%$

Concentration/mol dm^{-3}	COCl$_2$	CO	Cl$_2$
Initial	0.5/2 = 0.25	0	0
Change	$-x = 16\%$	$+x$	$+x$
Equilibrium	0.21	0.04	0.04

$$K_c = \frac{[CO][Cl_2]}{[COCl_2]} = \frac{0.04 \text{ mol dm}^{-3} \times 0.04 \text{ mol dm}^{-3}}{0.21 \text{ mol dm}^{-3}}$$

$$= 7.62 \times 10^{-3} \text{ mol dm}^{-3}$$

(19)

$$N_2(g) + O_2(g) \rightleftharpoons 2NO(g) : K_p = 2.5 \times 10^{-3} \text{ at } 2400 \text{ K}$$

Let p = partial pressure of NO at equilibrium

$$K_p = \frac{(p_{NO})^2}{(p_{N_2})(p_{O_2})} = 2.5 \times 10^{-3}$$

$$2.5 \times 10^{-3} = \frac{p^2}{0.5 \text{ atm} \times 0.05 \text{ atm}}$$

$$p^2 = 6.25 \times 10^{-5} \text{ atm}^2$$
$$p = 7.91 \times 10^{-3} \text{ atm}$$

(20)
(i)

$$CO(g) + H_2O(g) \rightleftharpoons CO_2(g) + H_2(g)$$

Concentration/mol dm^{-3}	CO	H$_2$O	CO$_2$	H$_2$
Initial	0.4	0.4	0	0
Change	$-x$	$-x$	$+x$	$+x$
Equilibrium	0.267	0.267	0.133	0.133

$$K_c = \frac{[CO_2][H_2]}{[CO][H_2O]} = \frac{(0.133 \text{ mol dm}^{-3})^2}{(0.267 \text{ mol dm}^{-3})^2} = 0.248$$

(ii)

$$K_p = K_c(RT)^{\Delta n}$$

where

Δn = number of moles of products − number of moles of reactants

$$= 2 - 2 = 0$$
$$K_p = K_c(RT)^0$$
$$K_p = K_c = 0.248$$

(21)
(a)

$$N_2O_4(g) \rightleftharpoons 2NO_2(g)$$

$$K_p = \frac{(p_{NO_2})^2}{p_{N_2O_4}} = ?$$

Inserting the values of the partial pressures into the equilibrium expression

$$K_p = \frac{(5 \times 10^4 \text{ Pa})^2}{5 \times 10^4 \text{ Pa}} = 5 \times 10^4 \text{ Pa}$$

50

(b)

Total pressure, $p = p_x + p_y$

where p_x and p_y are the partial pressures of N_2O_4 and NO_2 respectively.

$$2 \times 10^5 \text{ Pa} = p_x + p_y$$

$$p_y = 2 \times 10^5 - p_x$$

Inserting into the equilibrium expression

$$K_p = \frac{(p_{NO_2})^2}{p_{N_2O_4}} = 5 \times 10^4 \text{ Pa}$$

$$5 \times 10^4 \text{ Pa} = \frac{(2 \times 10^5 - p_x)^2}{p_x}$$

Solving the quadratic

$$p_x = 4.47 \times 10^3 \text{ Pa}$$

$$p_y = 1.96 \times 10^5 \text{ Pa}$$

(22)

$$K_p = K_c(RT)^{\Delta n} \quad \text{where } \Delta n = +1$$
$$K_c = K_p(RT)^{-\Delta n}$$
$$= 0.811 \text{ atm} \times (0.0821 \text{ atm dm}^3 \text{ K}^{-1} \text{ mol}^{-1} \times 523 \text{ K})^{-1}$$
$$= 1.89 \times 10^{-2} \text{ mol dm}^{-3}$$

(23)
(i)

$$N_2O_4(g) \rightleftharpoons 2NO_2(g)$$

$$K_p = \frac{(p_{NO_2})^2}{p_{N_2O_4}} = ?$$

Inserting the values of the partial pressures into the equilibrium expression

$$K_p = \frac{(0.31 \text{ atm})^2}{0.69 \text{ atm}}$$

$$= 0.1392 \text{ atm}$$

(ii)

Total pressure, $p = p_x + p_y$

where p_x and p_y are the partial pressures of N_2O_4 and NO_2 respectively.

$$10 \text{ atm} = p_x + p_y$$

$$p_y = 10 - p_x$$

Inserting into the equilibrium expression

$$K_p = \frac{(p_{NO_2})^2}{p_{N_2O_4}} = 0.1392 \text{ atm}$$

$$0.1392 \text{ atm} = \frac{(10 - p_x)^2}{p_x}$$

Solving the quadratic

$$p_x = 8.89 \text{ atm}$$

$$p_y = 1.11 \text{ atm}$$

(25)

$$N_2(g) + 3H_2(g) \rightleftharpoons 2NH_3(g)$$

Volume	N_2	H_2	NH_3
Initial	1.0	3.0	0
Equilibrium %	0.21175	0.63525	0.153

The volume % composition at equilibrium = mole fractions

Partial pressures

$$p_{N_2} = 0.21175 \times 10^5 \text{ Pa}$$
$$p_{H_2} = 0.63525 \times 10^5 \text{ Pa}$$
$$p_{NH_3} = 0.153 \times 10^5 \text{ Pa}$$

$$K_p = \frac{(p_{NH_3})^2}{(p_{N_2})(p_{H_2})^3}$$

$$= \frac{(0.153 \times 10^5 \text{ Pa})^2}{(0.21175 \times 10^5 \text{ Pa} \times (0.63525 \times 10^5 \text{ Pa})^3}$$

$$= 4.31 \times 10^{-11} \text{ Pa}^{-2}$$

(26)

$$N_2(g) + 3H_2(g) \rightleftharpoons 2NH_3(g)$$

Amount/mol	N_2	H_2	NH_3
Initial	1.0	3.0	0
Change	$-x$ -0.70	$-3x$ -2.10	$+2x$ 1.40
Equilibrium	0.30	0.90	1.40

Total amount of components $= (0.30 + 0.90 + 1.40)$ mol
$$= 2.60 \text{ mol}$$

Mole Fractions (X)

$$X_{N_2} = \frac{0.30}{2.60}$$

$$X_{H_2} = \frac{0.90}{2.60}$$

$$X_{NH_3} = \frac{1.40}{2.60}$$

Partial pressures

$$p_{N_2} = \frac{0.30}{2.60} \times 3.5 \times 10^7 \text{ Pa}$$

$$p_{H_2} = \frac{0.90}{2.60} \times 3.5 \times 10^7 \text{ Pa}$$

$$p_{NH_3} = \frac{1.40}{2.60} \times 3.5 \times 10^7 \text{ Pa}$$

$$K_p = \frac{(p_{NH_3})^2}{(p_{N_2})(p_{H_2})^3}$$

$$= \frac{(1.40/2.60)^2 \times (3.5 \times 10^7 \text{ Pa})^2}{(0.30/2.60) \times 3.5 \times 10^7 \text{ Pa} \times (0.90/2.40)^3 \times (3.5 \times 10^7 \text{ Pa})^3}$$

$$= 4.95 \times 10^{-14} \text{ Pa}^{-2}$$

(27)
(i)

$$I_2(g) \rightleftharpoons 2I(g)$$

Volume	I_2	I
Initial	1.0	0
Equilibrium	0.60	0.40

$$K_p = \frac{(p_I)^2}{p_{I_2}}$$
$$= \frac{(0.4 \times 10^5 \text{ Pa})^2}{0.6 \times 10^5 \text{ Pa}}$$
$$= 2.7 \times 10^4 \text{ Pa}$$

(ii)

Amount/vol	I_2	I
Equilibrium	0.80	0.20

Let p = total pressure

$$K_p = \frac{(p_I)^2}{p_{I_2}}$$
$$2.7 \times 10^4 \text{ Pa} = \frac{(0.2p)^2}{0.8p}$$
$$p = 5.4 \times 10^5 \text{ Pa}$$

CHAPTER 9.
ACIDS, BASES AND
IONIC EQUILIBRIUM

(5)

$$H_2O(l) \rightleftharpoons H^+(aq) + OH^-(aq)$$

$$K_c = \frac{[H^+][OH^-]}{[H_2O]}$$

$K_c[H_2O] = K_w = 1.0 \times 10^{-14} \, \text{mol}^2 \, \text{dm}^{-6}$ at 298 K
$K_w = [H^+][OH^-] = 1.0 \times 10^{-14} \, \text{mol}^2 \, \text{dm}^{-6}$ at 298 K
$[H_2O] = 55.6 \, \text{mol dm}^{-3}$

For pure water $[H^+] = [OH^-] = 1.0 \times 10^{-7} \, \text{mol dm}^{-3}$

Fraction of ionised water molecules $= \dfrac{[H^+]}{[H_2O]}$

$$= \frac{1.0 \times 10^{-7} \, \text{mol dm}^{-3}}{55.6 \, \text{mol dm}^{-3}}$$

$$= 1.80 \times 10^{-9}$$

(6) (b) (i)

$HCl(aq) \rightarrow H^+(aq) + Cl^-(aq)$
0.01 mol   0.01 mol

$$[H^+] = [HCl] = 0.01 \, \text{mol dm}^{-3}$$
$$pH = -\log[H^+]$$
$$= -\log 0.01$$

Using an electronic calculator

$$pH = -(-2) = +2$$

(ii)

$H_2SO_4(aq) \rightarrow 2H^+(aq) \quad + SO_4{}^{2-}(aq)$
0.01 mol 2×0.01 mol

$$[H^+] = 2[H_2SO_4] = 2 \times 0.01 \, \text{mol dm}^{-3}$$

$$pH = -\log[H^+]$$
$$= -\log(2 \times 0.01)$$
$$= -\log(0.02)$$
$$pH = -(-1.669)$$
$$= +1.669$$

(iii)

$$NaOH(aq) \rightarrow Na^+(aq) + OH^-(aq)$$
0.01 mol   0.01 mol

$$[OH^-] = [NaOH] = 0.01 \text{ mol dm}^{-3}$$
$$pOH = -\log[OH^-]$$
$$= -\log 0.01 = +2$$
$$pOH = -(-2)$$
$$= +2$$
$$pH = 14 - pOH = 14 - 2 = 12$$

(iv)

The amount of NaOH, $n = \dfrac{m}{M} = \dfrac{0.4 \text{ g}}{40 \text{ g mol}^{-1}} = 0.01 \text{ mol}$

The concentration of NaOH,

$$c = \frac{n}{V} = \frac{0.01 \text{ mol}}{0.25 \text{ dm}^3} = 0.04 \text{ mol dm}^{-3}$$

$$[OH^-] = [NaOH] = 0.04 \text{ mol dm}^{-3}$$
$$pOH = -\log[OH^-]$$
$$= -\log 0.04$$
$$= -(-1.39794)$$
$$= +1.39794$$
$$pH = 14 - pOH = 14 - 1.39794 = 12.6021$$

(v)

$$HCl(aq) + KOH(aq) \rightarrow KCl(aq) + H_2O(1)$$

Amount of HCl, $n = cV = 0.1 \text{ mol dm}^{-3} \times 0.06 \text{ dm}^3 = 0.006 \text{ mol}$

Amount of KOH, $n = cV = 0.1 \text{ mol dm}^{-3} \times 0.04 \text{ dm}^3 = 0.004 \text{ mol}$

Amount of excess HCl $= (0.006 - 0.004) \text{ mol} = 0.002 \text{ mol HCl}$

This excess HCl was in $(60 \text{ cm}^3 + 40 \text{ cm}^3)$ solution.

Concentration of excess HCl,

$$c = \frac{n}{V} = \frac{0.002 \text{ mol}}{0.1 \text{ dm}^3} = 0.02 \text{ mol dm}^{-3}$$

$$[H^+] = [HCl] = 0.02 \text{ mol dm}^{-3}$$
$$pH = -\log[H^+]$$
$$= -\log 0.02 = 1.699$$

(7)

$$H_2O(l) \rightleftharpoons H^+(aq) + OH^-(aq)$$

$$K_w = [H^+][OH^-] = 5.47 \times 10^{-14} \text{ at } 323 \text{ K}$$

For pure water

$$
\begin{aligned}
[H^+] &= [OH^-] \\
K_w &= [H^+]^2 = 5.47 \times 10^{-14} \\
[H^+]^2 &= 5.47 \times 10^{-14} \\
[H^+] &= \sqrt{5.47} \times 10^{-7} \\
&= 2.3388 \times 10^{-7} \\
pH &= -\log[H^+] \\
&= -\log(2.3388 \times 10^{-7}) \\
&= +6.6310
\end{aligned}
$$

(8)
(i)

$$
\begin{aligned}
pH &= -\log[H^+] \\
10.0 &= -\log[H^+]
\end{aligned}
$$

Using an electronic calculator

$$
\begin{aligned}
[H^+] &= \text{antilog}(-10.0) \\
&= 1.0 \times 10^{-10} \text{ mol dm}^{-3}
\end{aligned}
$$

(ii)

$$
\begin{aligned}
pH &= -\log[H^+] \\
9.40 &= -\log[H^+]
\end{aligned}
$$

Using an electronic calculator

$$
\begin{aligned}
[H^+] &= \text{antilog}(-9.40) \\
&= 3.9811 \times 10^{-10} \text{ mol dm}^{-3}
\end{aligned}
$$

(iii)

$$
\begin{aligned}
[H^+] &= \text{antilog}(-1.40) \\
&= 0.0398 \text{ mol dm}^{-3}
\end{aligned}
$$

(iv)

$$
\begin{aligned}
[H^+] &= \text{antilog}(-4.82) \\
&= 1.5136 \times 10^{-5} \text{ mol dm}^{-3}
\end{aligned}
$$

(v)

$$
\begin{aligned}
[H^+] &= \text{antilog}(-0.05) \\
&= 0.8913 \text{ mol dm}^{-3}
\end{aligned}
$$

(vi)

$$
\begin{aligned}
[H^+] &= \text{antilog}(-7.7) \\
&= 1.9952 \times 10^{-8} \text{ mol dm}^{-3}
\end{aligned}
$$

(9)
(ii)

$$C_2H_5COOH(l) + H_2O(l) \rightleftharpoons C_2H_5COO^-(aq) + H_3O^+(aq)$$

$$K_d = \frac{[C_2H_5COO^-][H_3O^+]}{[C_2H_5COOH]} = 1.35 \times 10^{-5} \text{ at } 298 \text{ K}$$

The concentration of the hydronium ions $[H_3O^+]$, can be written as $[H^+]$

Let $x =$ the molar change in concentration of each species.

Concentration/mol dm^{-3}	C_2H_5COOH	$C_2H_5COO^-$	H^+
Initial	0.1	0	0
Change	$-x$	$+x$	$+x$
Equilibrium	$0.1 - x$	$+x$	$+x$

Inserting into the equilibrium expression

$$K_d = \frac{x \cdot x}{0.1 - x} = 1.35 \times 10^{-5}$$

As x is small it can be neglected compared with 0.1, i.e. $0.1 - x \approx 0.1$

$$\frac{x \cdot x}{0.1} = 1.35 \times 10^{-5}$$

$$x^2 = 0.1 \times 1.35 \times 10^{-5}$$
$$= 1.35 \times 10^{-6}$$
$$x = \sqrt{1.35} \times 10^{-3}$$
$$= 1.1619 \times 10^{-3}$$

As $x = [H^+]$

$$pH = -\log[H^+]$$
$$= -\log(1.1619 \times 10^{-3})$$
$$= +2.9348$$

(10)

$$HIO_3(aq) \rightleftharpoons H^+(aq) + IO_3^-(aq)$$

$$K_a = \frac{[H^+][IO_3^-]}{[HIO_3]} = 0.17 \text{ mol } dm^{-3} \text{ at } 298 \text{ K}$$

Concentration/mol dm^{-3}	HIO_3	H^+	IO_3^-
Initial	0.01	0	0
Change	$-x$	$+x$	$+x$
Equilibrium	$0.01 - x$	$+x$	$+x$

Inserting into the equilibrium expression

$$K_d = \frac{x \cdot x}{0.01 - x} = 0.17$$

As x is small it can be neglected compared with 0.01, i.e. $0.01 - x \approx 0.01$

$$\frac{x \cdot x}{0.01} = 0.17$$

$$x^2 = 0.01 \times 0.17$$
$$= 1.7 \times 10^{-3}$$
$$x = \sqrt{17 \times 10^{-4}}$$
$$= 4.123 \times 10^{-2}$$

As $x = [H^+]$

$$pH = -\log[H^+]$$
$$= -\log(4.123 \times 10^{-2})$$
$$= +1.3848$$

(11)

$$HNO_2(aq) \rightleftharpoons H^+(aq) + NO_2^-(aq)$$

$$K_a = \frac{[H^+][NO_2^-]}{[HNO_2]} = 4.7 \times 10^{-4} \text{ mol dm}^{-3} \text{ at } 298 \text{ K}$$

Concentration/mol dm^{-3}	HNO$_2$	H$^+$	NO$_2^-$
Initial	0.02	0	0
Change	$-x$	$+x$	$+x$
Equilibrium	$0.02 - x$	$+x$	$+x$

Inserting into the equilibrium expression

$$K_d = \frac{x \cdot x}{0.02 - x} = 4.7 \times 10^{-4}$$

As x is small it can be neglected compared with 0.02, i.e. $0.02 - x \approx 0.02$

$$\frac{x \cdot x}{0.02} = 4.7 \times 10^{-4}$$

$$x^2 = 0.02 \times 4.7 \times 10^{-4}$$
$$= 9.4 \times 10^{-6}$$
$$x = \sqrt{9.4 \times 10^{-3}}$$
$$= 3.0659 \times 10^{-3}$$

As $x = [H^+]$

$$pH = -\log[H^+]$$
$$= -\log(3.0659 \times 10^{-3})$$
$$= +2.5134$$

(12)
(ii)

$$NH_3(aq) + H_2O(aq) \rightleftharpoons NH_4^+(aq) + OH^-(aq)$$

$$K_d = \frac{[NH_4^+][OH^-]}{[NH_3]} = 1.75 \times 10^{-5} \text{ at } 298 \text{ K}$$

Let $x =$ the molar change in concentration of each species

Concentration/mol dm^{-3}	NH_3	NH_4^+	OH^-
Initial	0.4	0	0
Change	$-x$	$+x$	$+x$
Equilibrium	$0.4 - x$	$+x$	$+x$

Inserting into the equilibrium expression

$$K_b = \frac{x \cdot x}{0.4 - x} = 1.75 \times 10^{-5}$$

As x is small it can be neglected compared with 0.2, i.e. $0.4 - x \approx 0.4$

$$\frac{x \cdot x}{0.4} = 1.75 \times 10^{-5}$$

$$\begin{aligned}
x^2 &= 0.4 \times 1.75 \times 10^{-5} \\
&= 0.7 \times 10^{-5} \\
&= 7.0 \times 10^{-6} \\
x &= \sqrt{7.0} \times 10^{-3} \\
&= 2.6458 \times 10^{-3}
\end{aligned}$$

As $x = [OH^-]$,

$$\begin{aligned}
pOH &= -\log[OH^-] \\
&= -\log(2.6458 \times 10^{-3}) \\
&= +2.5775
\end{aligned}$$

$$pH = 14 - 2.5775 = 11.4225$$

(13)

$$Mor(aq) + H_2O \rightleftharpoons Mor - H^+(aq) + OH^-(aq)$$

$$K_b = \frac{[Mor - H^+][OH^-]}{[Mor]} = 1.60 \times 10^{-6} \text{ mol dm}^{-3} \text{ at } 298 \text{ K}$$

Let $x =$ the molar change in concentration of each species.

Concentration/mol dm^{-3}	Mor	Mor $- H^+$	OH^-
Initial	0.01	0	0
Change	$-x$	$+x$	$+x$
Equilibrium	$0.01 - x$	$+x$	$+x$

Inserting into the equilibrium expression

$$K_b = \frac{x \cdot x}{0.01 - x} = 1.6 \times 10^{-6}$$

As x is small it can be neglected compared with 0.01, i.e. $0.01 - x \approx 0.01$

$$\frac{x \cdot x}{0.01} = 1.60 \times 10^{-6}$$

$$x^2 = 0.01 \times 1.60 \times 10^{-6}$$
$$= 1.6 \times 10^{-8}$$
$$x = \sqrt{1.6 \times 10^{-4}}$$
$$= 1.2649 \times 10^{-4}$$

As $x = [OH^-]$,

$$pOH = -\log[OH^-]$$
$$= -\log(1.2649 \times 10^{-4})$$
$$= +3.8979$$
$$pH = 14 - 3.8979 = 10.1021$$

(14)

$$CH_3COOH(1) + H_2O(1) \rightleftharpoons CH_3COO^-(aq) + H_3O^+(aq)$$

$$K_d = \frac{[CH_3COO^-][H_3O^+]}{[CH_3COOH]} = ?$$

Concentration/mol dm^{-3}	CH$_3$COOH	CH$_3$COO$^-$	H$^+$
Initial	0.1	0	0
Change	$-x$ -0.0013	$+x$ $+0.0013$	$+x$ $+0.0013$
Equilibrium	0.0987	0.0013	0.0013

Inserting into the equilibrium expression

$$K_d = \frac{[CH_3COO^-][H_3O^+]}{[CH_3COOH]} = \frac{(0.0013 \text{ mol dm}^{-3})^2}{0.0987 \text{ mol dm}^{-3}}$$
$$= 1.71 \times 10^{-5} \text{ mol dm}^{-3}$$

(15)

$$CH_3COOH(1) + H_2O(1) \rightleftharpoons CH_3COO^-(aq) + H_3O^+(aq)$$

$$K_d = \frac{[CH_3COO^-][H_3O^+]}{[CH_3COOH]} = ?$$

$$[CH_3COO^-] = [H_3O^+] = [H^+]$$

$$K_d = \frac{[H^+]^2}{[CH_3COOH]}$$

$$pH = -\log[H^+]$$
$$[H^+] = \text{antilog}(-pH)$$
$$= \text{antilog}(-3.40)$$
$$= 3.9811 \times 10^{-4}\,\text{mol dm}^{-3}$$

$$K_d = \frac{[H^+]^2}{[CH_3COOH]} = \frac{(3.9811 \times 10^{-4}\,\text{mol dm}^{-3})^2}{0.1\,\text{mol dm}^{-3}}$$

$$= 1.58 \times 10^{-6}\,\text{mol dm}^{-3}$$

(16)

$$CH_3COOH(1) + H_2O(1) \rightleftharpoons CH_3COO^-(aq) + H_3O^+(aq)$$

$$K_d = \frac{[CH_3COO^-][H_3O^+]}{[CH_3COOH]} = 1.75 \times 10^{-5} \text{ at } 198\,K$$

$$[CH_3COO^-] = [H_3O^+] = [H^+]$$

$$K_d = \frac{[H^+]^2}{[CH_3COOH]}$$

$$pH = -\log[H^+]$$
$$[H^+] = \text{antilog}(-pH)$$
$$= \text{antilog}(-2.0)$$
$$= 0.01\,\text{mol dm}^{-3}$$
$$[H^+]^2 = K_d[CH_3COOH]$$

$$(0.01\,\text{mol dm}^{-3})^2 = 1.75 \times 10^{-5}\,\text{mol dm}^{-3}[CH_3COOH]$$

$$[CH_3COOH] = 5.7143\,\text{mol dm}^{-3}$$

(17)

$$HC_3H_5O_3 \rightleftharpoons H^+ + C_3H_5O_3{}^-$$

$$K_d = \frac{[H^+][C_3H_5O_3^-]}{[HC_3H_5O_3]}$$

$$pH = -\log[H^+]$$
$$[H^+] = \text{antilog}(-pH)$$
$$= \text{antilog}(-2.75)$$
$$= 1.7783 \times 10^{-3}\,\text{mol dm}^{-3}$$
$$[H^+] = [C_3H_5O_3{}^-]$$

$$K_d = \frac{[H^+]^2}{[HC_3H_5O_3]} = \frac{(1.7783 \times 10^{-3}\,\text{mol dm}^{-3})^2}{0.025\,\text{mol dm}^{-3}}$$

$$= 1.2649 \times 10^{-4}\,\text{mol dm}^{-3}$$

(21)

Let HA = weak monobasic acid

$$HA \rightleftharpoons H^+ + A^-$$

$$K_a = \frac{[H^+][A^-]}{[HA]} = ?$$

$$pH = -\log[H^+]$$
$$[H^+] = antilog(-pH)$$
$$= antilog(-3.70)$$
$$= 1.9953 \times 10^{-4} \text{ mol dm}^{-3}$$
$$[H^+] = [A^-]$$

$$K_d = \frac{[H^+]^2}{[HA]} = \frac{(1.9953 \times 10^{-4} \text{ mol dm}^{-3})^2}{1.0 \text{ mol dm}^{-3}}$$

$$= 3.9811 \times 10^{-8} \text{ mol dm}^{-3}$$

(22)

$$H_2O \rightleftharpoons H^+(aq) + OH^-(aq)$$

$$K_w = [H^+][OH^-] = 9.55 \times 10^{-14} \text{ mol}^2 \text{ dm}^{-6} \text{ at } 333 \text{ K}$$
$$[H^+] = antilog(-pH)$$
$$= antilog(-6.90)$$
$$= 1.2589 \times 10^{-7} \text{ mol dm}^{-3}$$

$$[OH^-] = \frac{K_w}{[H^+]} = \frac{9.55 \times 10^{-14} \text{ mol}^2 \text{ dm}^{-6}}{1.2589 \times 10^{-7} \text{ mol dm}^{-3}}$$

$$= 7.5860 \times 10^{-7} \text{ mol dm}^{-3}$$

As $[OH^-] > [H^+]$ the solution is basic.

CHAPTER 10. OXIDATION AND REDUCTION

(10)

$$MnO_4^- + 8H^+ + 5Fe^{2+} \rightarrow Mn^{2+} + 5Fe^{3+} + 4H_2O$$

$$\frac{c_A V_A}{a} = \frac{c_B V_B}{b} \quad \text{where } a = 1 \text{ and } b = 5$$

$$\frac{c_A \times 25.0 \text{ cm}^3}{1} = \frac{0.1 \text{ mol dm}^{-3} \times 24.5 \text{ cm}^3}{5}$$

$$c_A = \frac{0.1 \text{ mol dm}^{-3} \times 24.5 \text{ cm}^3}{25.0 \text{ cm}^3 \times 5}$$

Therefore, c_A, the concentration of $KMnO_4 = 0.0196 \text{ mol dm}^{-3}$

(11)
(v)

$$MnO_4^- + 8H^+ + 5Fe^{2+} \rightarrow Mn^{2+} + 5Fe^{3+} + 4H_2O$$

$$\frac{c_A V_A}{a} = \frac{c_B V_B}{b} \quad \text{where } a = 1 \text{ and } b = 5$$

$$\frac{c_A \times 24.8 \text{ cm}^3}{1} = \frac{0.1 \text{ mol dm}^{-3} \times 25.0 \text{ cm}^3}{5}$$

$$c_A = \frac{0.1 \text{ mol dm}^{-3} \times 25.0 \text{ cm}^3}{24.8 \text{ cm}^3 \times 5}$$

Therefore, c_A, the concentration of $KMnO_4 = 0.0202 \text{ mol dm}^{-3}$

(12)

$$Fe(s) + H_2SO_4(aq) \rightarrow FeSO_4(aq) + H_2(g)$$
$$2.90 \text{ g}$$
$$MnO_4^- + 8H^+ + 5Fe^{2+} \rightarrow Mn^{2+} + 5Fe^{3+} + 4H_2O$$

$$\frac{c_A V_A}{a} = \frac{c_B V_B}{b} \quad \text{where } a = 1 \text{ and } b = 5$$

$$\frac{0.02 \times 24.8 \text{ cm}^3}{1} = \frac{c_B \times 25.0 \text{ cm}^3}{5}$$

$$c_B = \frac{0.02 \text{ mol dm}^{-3} \times 24.8 \text{ cm}^3 \times 5}{25.0 \text{ cm}^3}$$

c_B, the concentration of $Fe^{2+} = 0.0992$ mol dm^{-3}
$$= 0.0496 \text{ mol}/500 \text{ cm}^3$$
$$= 0.0496 \text{ mol} \times 56 \text{ g mol}^{-1} Fe^{2+}/500 \text{ cm}^3$$
$$= 2.7776 \text{ g } Fe^{2+}$$

$$\% \text{ Fe in sample} = \frac{2.7776}{2.90} \times 100\% = 95.8\%$$

(13)
(iii)

$$2KMnO_4 + 5(COOH)_2 + 3H_2SO_4 \rightarrow K_2SO_4 + 2MnSO_4 + 8H_2O + 10CO_2$$

$$\frac{c_A V_A}{a} = \frac{c_B V_B}{b} \quad \text{where } a = 2 \text{ and } b = 5$$

$$\frac{0.022 \times 20.0 \text{ cm}^3}{2} = \frac{c_B \times 25.0 \text{ cm}^3}{5}$$

$$c_B = \frac{0.022 \text{ mol dm}^{-3} \times 20.0 \text{ cm}^3 \times 5}{25.00 \text{ cm}^3 \times 2}$$

c_B, the concentration of anhydrous $C_2H_2O_4 = 0.044$ mol dm^{-3}
$$= 0.022 \text{ mol}/500 \text{ cm}^3$$
$$= 0.022 \text{ mol} \times 90 \text{ g mol}^{-1}/500 \text{ cm}^3$$
$$= 1.98 \text{ g } C_2H_4O_4/500 \text{ cm}^3$$

Mass of water of crystallisation = Mass of crystalline $C_2H_2O_4$ − Mass of anhydrous $C_2H_2O_4$
$$2.75 \text{ g} - 1.98 \text{ g} = 0.77 \text{ g}$$

(a)

$$\% \text{ Water of crystallisation} = \frac{\text{Mass of water of crystallisation}}{\text{Mass of crystalline } C_2H_2O_4} \times 100\%$$

$$= \frac{0.77 \text{ g}}{2.75 \text{ g}} \times 100\% = 28.0\%$$

(b)

$$\text{Amount of water} = \frac{m}{M} = \frac{0.77 \text{ g}}{18.0 \text{ g mol}^{-1}} = 0.0423 \text{ mol}$$

$$x = \frac{\text{Amount of water}}{\text{Amount of anhydrous } C_2H_2O_4} = \frac{0.0423 \text{ mol}}{0.022 \text{ mol}} = 1.94$$

As x must be an integer the correct value for x is 2.

(14)

$$2KMnO_4 + 5(COOH)_2 + 3H_2SO_4 \rightarrow K_2SO_4 + 2MnSO_4 + 8H_2O + 10CO_2$$

$$\frac{c_A V_A}{a} = \frac{c_B V_B}{b} \quad \text{where } a = 2 \text{ and } b = 5$$

$$\frac{0.15 \times 28.0 \text{ cm}^3}{2} = \frac{c_B \times 25.0 \text{ cm}^3}{5}$$

$$c_B = \frac{0.15 \text{ mol dm}^{-3} \times 28.0 \text{ cm}^3 \times 5}{25.00 \text{ cm}^3 \times 2}$$

$$= 0.42 \text{ mol dm}^{-3}$$
$$= 0.42 \text{ mol} \times 90 \text{ g mol}^{-1} \text{ dm}^{-3}$$
$$= 37.8 \text{ g dm}^{-3} \text{ C}_2\text{H}_4\text{O}_4$$

(15)

$$2KMnO_4 + 10KI + 8H_2O \rightarrow 6K_2SO_4 + 2MnSO_4 + 8H_2O + 5I_2$$

$$2Na_2S_2O_3 + I_2 \rightarrow 2NaI + Na_2S_4O_6$$

Overall, *Two mol KMnO$_4$ $\equiv$ Five mol I$_2$ $\equiv$ Ten mol Na$_2$S$_2$O$_3$*

$$\frac{c_A V_A}{a} = \frac{c_B V_B}{b} \quad \text{where } c_A = \text{concentration of KMnO}_4$$

$$c_B = \text{concentration of Na}_2\text{S}_2\text{O}_3$$
$$a = 2 \text{ and } b = 10$$

$$\frac{0.02 \times 25.00 \text{ cm}^3}{2} = \frac{c_B \times 19.50 \text{ cm}^3}{10}$$

$$c_B = \frac{0.02 \text{ mol dm}^{-3} \times 25.00 \text{ cm}^3 \times 10}{19.50 \text{ cm}^3 \times 2}$$

c_B, the concentration of thiosulphate $= 0.1282 \text{ mol dm}^{-3}$

(16)

$$2Na_2S_2O_3 + I_2 \rightarrow 2NaI + Na_2S_4O_6$$

(a)

$$\frac{c_A V_A}{a} = \frac{c_B V_B}{b} \quad \text{where } a = 2 \text{ and } b = 1$$

$$\frac{0.12 \times 22.2 \text{ cm}^3}{2} = \frac{c_B \times 25.0 \text{ cm}^3}{1}$$

$$c_B = \frac{0.12 \text{ mol dm}^{-3} \times 22.2 \text{ cm}^3}{25.0 \text{ cm}^3 \times 2}$$

c_B, the concentration of iodine $= 0.0533 \text{ mol dm}^{-3}$

(b)

Concentration in g dm^{-3} $= 0.0533 \text{ mol} \times 254 \text{ g mol}^{-1} \text{ dm}^{-3}$
$$= 13.54 \text{ g dm}^{-3} \text{ I}_2$$

(17)
(iv)

$$MnO_4^- + 8H^+ + 5Fe^{2+} \rightarrow Mn^{2+} + 5Fe^{3+} + 4H_2O$$

$$\frac{c_A V_A}{a} = \frac{c_B V_B}{b} \quad \text{where } a = 1 \text{ and } b = 5$$

$$\frac{0.02 \text{ mol dm}^{-3} \times 18.1 \text{ cm}^3}{1} = \frac{c_B \times 20.0 \text{ cm}^3}{5}$$

$$c_B = \frac{0.02 \text{ mol dm}^{-3} \times 18.1 \text{ cm}^3 \times 5}{20.0 \text{ cm}^3}$$

c_B, the concentration of $FeSO_4 = 0.0905$ mol dm^{-3}
$$= 0.022625 \text{ mol}/250 \text{ cm}^3$$
$$= 0.022625 \text{ mol} \times 152 \text{ g mol}^{-1}/250 \text{ cm}^3$$
$$= 3.439 \text{ g}/250 \text{ cm}^3$$

(v)

Mass of water = mass of anhydrous $FeSO_4$ − mass of crystalline $FeSO_4$
$$= 6.25 \text{ g} - 3.439 \text{ g} = 2.811 \text{ g H}_2O$$

$$\% \text{ water of crystallisation} = \frac{2.811}{6.25} \times 100\% = 45\%$$

(vi)

Amount of water $= \dfrac{m}{M} = \dfrac{2.811 \text{ g}}{18.0 \text{ g mol}^{-1}} = 0.1562$ mol

$$x = \frac{\text{Amount of water}}{\text{Amount of anhydrous } FeSO_4} = \frac{0.1562 \text{ mol}}{0.022625 \text{ mol}} = 6.9$$

As x must be an integer the correct value for x is 7.

(18)

$$MnO_4^- + 8H^+ + 5Fe^{2+} \rightarrow Mn^{2+} + 5Fe^{3+} + 4H_2O$$

$\dfrac{c_A V_A}{a} = \dfrac{c_B V_B}{b}$ where $a = 1$ and $b = 5$

$$\frac{0.02 \text{ mol dm}^{-3} \times 20.0 \text{ cm}^3}{1} = \frac{c_B \times 25.0 \text{ cm}^3}{5}$$

$$c_B = \frac{0.02 \text{ mol dm}^{-3} \times 20.0 \text{ cm}^3 \times 5}{25.0 \text{ cm}^3}$$

c_B, the concentration of $FeSO_4 = 0.08$ mol dm^{-3}
$$= 0.02 \text{ mol}/250 \text{ cm}^3$$
$$= 0.02 \text{ mol} \times 152 \text{ g mol}^{-1}/250 \text{ cm}^3$$
$$= 3.04 \text{ g } FeSO_4/250 \text{ cm}^3$$

(v)

Mass of water = mass of anhydrous $FeSO_4$ − mass of crystalline $FeSO_4$
$$= 5.5 \text{ g} - 3.04 \text{ g} = 2.46 \text{ g H}_2O$$

$$\% \text{ water of crystallisation} = \frac{2.46}{5.5} \times 100\% = 44.7\%$$

CHAPTER 12. WATER—PROPERTIES, TREATMENT AND ANALYSIS

(11)

$$1 \text{ mol } O_2 \equiv 2 \text{ mol } I_2 \equiv 4 \text{ mol } Na_2S_2O_3 \text{ i.e. } 1 \text{ mol } O_2 \equiv 4 \text{ mol } Na_2S_2O_3$$

Initial D.O. determination

$$\frac{c_A V_A}{a} = \frac{c_B V_B}{b}$$

$$\frac{c_A \times 300 \text{ cm}^3}{1} = \frac{0.02 \text{ mol dm}^{-3} \times 18.0 \text{ cm}^3}{4}$$

$$c_A = \frac{0.02 \times 18.0}{4 \times 300} \text{ mol dm}^{-3} \text{ O}_2$$

$$= 3 \times 10^{-4} \text{ mol dm}^{-3} \text{ O}_2$$

D.O. determination after 5 days

$$\frac{c_A V_A}{a} = \frac{c_B V_B}{b}$$

$$\frac{c_A \times 300 \text{ cm}^3}{1} = \frac{0.02 \text{ mol dm}^{-3} \times 6.0 \text{ cm}^3}{4}$$

$$c_A = \frac{0.02 \times 6.0}{4 \times 300} \text{ mol dm}^{-3} \text{ O}_2$$

$$= 1 \times 10^{-4} \text{ mol dm}^{-3} \text{ O}_2$$

Difference in D.O. after five days = B.O.D.

$$= (3 \times 10^{-4} - 1 \times 10^{-4}) \text{ mol dm}^{-3} \text{ O}_2$$
$$= 2 \times 10^{-4} \times 32 \text{ g mol}^{-1} \text{ mol dm}^{-3} \text{ O}_2$$
$$= 6.4 \text{ mg dm}^{-3} \text{ O}_2$$
$$= 6.4 \text{ ppm dissolved O}_2$$

(15)

Mass of suspended solids $= (1.25 - 0.80) \text{ g} = 0.45 \text{ g}$

Concentration of suspended solids $= \dfrac{0.45 \text{ g}}{2 \text{ dm}^3} = 0.225 \text{ g dm}^{-3}$

$= 225 \text{ mg dm}^{-3}$

$= 225 \text{ ppm}$

Mass of dissolved solids $= 0.75 \text{ g}$

Concentration of dissolved solids $= \dfrac{0.75 \text{ g}}{0.5 \text{ dm}^3} = 1.5 \text{ g dm}^{-3}$

$= 1500 \text{ mg dm}^{-3}$

$= 1500 \text{ ppm}$

(16)

$1 \text{ mol } O_2 \equiv 2 \text{ mol } I_2 \equiv 4 \text{ mol } Na_2S_2O_3$ i.e. $1 \text{ mol } O_2 \equiv 4 \text{ mol } Na_2S_2O_3$

$$\frac{c_A V_A}{a} = \frac{c_B V_B}{b}$$

$$\frac{c_A \times 100 \text{ cm}^3}{1} = \frac{0.02 \text{ mol dm}^{-3} \times 4.5 \text{ cm}^3}{4}$$

$$c_A = \frac{0.02 \times 4.5}{4 \times 100} \text{ mol dm}^{-3} \, O_2$$

$= 2.25 \times 10^{-4} \text{ mol dm}^{-3} \, O_2$

$= 2.25 \times 10^{-4} \text{ mol dm}^{-3} \times 32 \text{ g mol}^{-1} \, O_2$

$= 7.2 \times 10^{-3} \text{ g dm}^{-3} \, O_2$

$= 7.2 \text{ mg dm}^{-3} \, O_2$

$= 7.2 \text{ ppm } O_2$

(17)

$1 \text{ mol } Ca^{2+} \equiv 1 \text{ mol EDTA}$

$$\frac{c_A V_A}{a} = \frac{c_B V_B}{b}$$

$$\frac{c_A \times 50 \text{ cm}^3}{1} = \frac{0.01 \text{ mol dm}^{-3} \times 20 \text{ cm}^3}{1}$$

$$c_A = \frac{0.01 \text{ mol dm}^{-3} \times 20 \text{ cm}^3}{50 \text{ cm}^3}$$

$= 0.004 \text{ mol dm}^{-3} \, CaCO_3$

$= 0.004 \times 100 \text{ g dm}^{-3} \, CaCO_3$

$= 0.4 \text{ g dm}^{-3} \, CaCO_3$

$= 400 \text{ mg dm}^{-3} \, CaCO_3$

$= 400 \text{ ppm } CaCO_3$

(19)

(g)

1 mol $O_2 \equiv 2$ mol $I_2 \equiv 4$ mol $Na_2S_2O_3$ i.e. 1 mol $O_2 \equiv 4$ mol $Na_2S_2O_3$

$$\frac{c_A V_A}{a} = \frac{c_B V_B}{b}$$

$$\frac{c_A \times 100 \text{ cm}^3}{1} = \frac{0.02 \text{ mol dm}^{-3} \times 4.0 \text{ cm}^3}{4}$$

$$c_A = \frac{0.02 \times 4.0}{4 \times 100} \text{ mol dm}^{-3} O_2$$

$$= 2.0 \times 10^{-4} \text{ mol dm}^{-3} O_2$$
$$= 2.0 \times 10^{-4} \text{ mol dm}^{-3} \times 32 \text{ g mol}^{-1} O_2$$
$$= 6.4 \times 10^{-3} \text{ g dm}^{-3} O_2$$
$$= 6.4 \text{ mg dm}^{-3} O_2$$
$$= 6.4 \text{ ppm } O_2$$

(20)

$$1 \text{ mol Ca}^{2+} \equiv 1 \text{ mol EDTA}$$

$$\frac{c_A V_A}{a} = \frac{c_B V_B}{b}$$

$$\frac{c_A \times 50 \text{ cm}^3}{1} = \frac{0.01 \text{ mol dm}^{-3} \times 25 \text{ cm}^3}{1}$$

$$c_A = \frac{0.01 \text{ mol dm}^{-3} \times 25 \text{ cm}^3}{50 \text{ cm}^3}$$

$$= 0.005 \text{ mol dm}^{-3} CaCO_3$$
$$= 0.005 \times 100 \text{ g dm}^{-3} CaCO_3$$
$$= 0.5 \text{ g dm}^{-3} CaCO_3$$
$$= 500 \text{ mg dm}^{-3} CaCO_3$$
$$= 500 \text{ ppm } CaCO_3$$

CHAPTER 13. NON-METALS 2. CARBON, NITROGEN AND SULPHUR

(16)
Determination of the amount of unreacted hydrochloric acid

$$H_2SO_4 + 2NaOH \rightarrow Na_2SO_4 + 2H_2O$$

Using $\dfrac{c_A V_A}{a} = \dfrac{c_B V_B}{b}$

$$\frac{c_A \times 25\ cm^3}{1} = \frac{0.1\ mol\ dm^{-3} \times 22.2\ cm^3}{2}$$

c_A, the concentration of unreacted $H_2SO_4 = 0.0444\ mol\ dm^{-3}\ H_2SO_4$

The amount of unreacted H_2SO_4, $n = cV$
$$= 0.0888\ mol\ dm^{-3} \times 0.25\ dm^3$$
$$= 0.0111\ mol\ H_2SO_4$$

The amount of H_2SO_4 initially, $n = cV$
$$= 0.5\ mol\ dm^{-3} \times 0.05\ dm^3$$
$$= 0.025\ mol\ HCl$$

Amount of H_2SO_4 which reacted with Ammonia
$$= \text{Amount of } H_2SO_4 \text{ initially} - \text{amount of unreacted } H_2SO_4$$
$$= 0.025 - 0.0111\ mol$$
$$= 0.0139\ mol\ H_2SO_4$$

Amount of Ammonia in Fertiliser

$$2NH_3 + H_2SO_4 \rightarrow (NH_4)_2SO_4$$

2 mol NH_3 reacts with 1 mol H_2SO_4 to form 2 mol NH_4^+ ion
2×0.0139 mol NH_3 reacts with 0.0139 mol H_2SO_4 to form 2×0.0139 mol NH_4^+
i.e. there are 2×0.0139 mol NH_4^+ ions in 1.60 g of fertiliser.
Now,

$$m = nM = 0.0278\ mol \times 18\ g\ mol^{-1}\ NH_4^+ \text{ ions}$$
$$= 0.5004\ g\ NH_4^+$$

Now,

$$\% \text{ Ammonium Ion} = \frac{\text{Mass of } NH_4^+}{\text{Mass of Fertiliser}} \times 100\%$$

$$= \frac{0.5004\ g}{1.60\ g} \times 100\% = 31.3\%$$

(17)

$$\%\text{N} = \frac{3 \times M(\text{N})}{M((\text{NH}_4)_3\text{PO}_4)} \times 100\% = \frac{42}{149} \times 100\%$$

$$= 28.2\%$$

$$\%\text{N} = \frac{2 \times M(\text{N})}{M((\text{NH}_4)_2\text{SO}_4)} \times 100\% = \frac{28}{132} \times 100\%$$

$$= 21.2\%$$

CHAPTER 15. ELECTROCHEMISTRY AND THE ACTIVITY SERIES

(13)
(iii)
The electrode reactions are

Cathode: $Ag^+ + e^- \rightarrow Ag$
Anode: $O^{2-} \rightarrow \frac{1}{2}O_2 + e^-$

$$\text{Number of Faradays} = \frac{965}{96500} = 0.01 \text{ F}$$

1 mol Ag^+ + 1 mol e^-(1F) $\rightarrow$ 1 mol Ag
0.01 mol Ag^+ + 0.01 mol e^-(0.01 F) $\rightarrow$ 0.01 mol Ag

$m = nM = 0.01 \text{ mol} \times 108 \text{ g mol}^{-1} \text{ Ag}$
$\qquad = 1.08 \text{ g Ag}$

1 mol $O^{2-} \rightarrow \frac{1}{2}$ mol O_2 + 1 mol e^-(1F)
0.01 mol $O^{2-} \rightarrow$ 0.005 mol O_2 + 0.01 mol e^-(0.01 F)

$V = nV_m = 0.005 \text{ mol} \times 22.4 \text{ dm}^3 \text{ mol}^{-1} \text{ O}_2$
$\qquad = 0.112 \text{ dm}^3 \text{ O}_2$

(14)
(i)

$$1.0 \text{ mol Na}^+ + 1 \text{ mol } e^-(1\text{F}) \rightarrow 1 \text{ mol Na}$$

$\quad$ 1F = 96500 C

(ii)

$$1.0 \text{ mol Cu}^{2+} + 2 \text{ mol } e^-(2\text{F}) \rightarrow 1 \text{ mol Cu}$$

$\quad$ 2F = 193000 C

(iii)

0.23 g Na = 0.01 mol Na

1 mol Na^+ + 1 mol e^-(1F) $\rightarrow$ 1 mol Na
0.01 mol Na^+ + 0.01 mol e^-(0.01 F) $\rightarrow$ 0.01 mol Na

$\quad$ 0.01 F = 965 C

(iv)

1.8 g H_2O = 0.1 mol H_2O

1.0 mol $H_2O \rightarrow \frac{1}{2}$ mol O_2 + 2 mol e^-(2F)
0.1 mol $H_2O \rightarrow 0.05$ mol O_2 + 0.2 mol e^-(0.2 F)

0.2F = 19300 C

(v)

71 g of Cl^- = 2.0 mol Cl^-

2.0 mol $Cl^- \rightarrow 1.0$ mol Cl_2 + 2.0 mol e^-(2F)

2F = 193000 C

(15)
Cathode reaction:

$$Ni^{2+} + 2e^- \rightarrow Ni$$

2F(193000 C) $\rightarrow$ 1 mol Ni

Number of Coulombs = Current $\times$ Time = 1.25 amps $\times$ 1500 s
$$= 1875 \text{ C}$$

131000 C $\rightarrow$ 1 mol Ni (58.7 g)

1875 C $\rightarrow \dfrac{58.7 \text{ g} \times 1875}{193000} = 0.57$ g Ni

(16)

$Fe^{3+} + 3e^- \rightarrow Fe$
3×96500 C $\rightarrow 56$ g

$\dfrac{3 \times 96500 \times 10 \text{ C}}{56} \rightarrow 10$ g

Let t = time

$\dfrac{3 \times 96500 \times 10 \text{ C}}{56} = 1.5t$ Coulombs

$t = 34464$ s = 574.4 min.

(17)
The electrode reactions are

Cathode: $Pb^{2+} + 2e^- \rightarrow Pb$
Anode: $2Br^- \rightarrow Br_2 + 2e^-$

Number of Faradays $= \dfrac{0.5 \times 965}{96500} = 0.005$ F

1 mol Pb^{2+} + 2 mol e^-(1F) $\rightarrow$ 1 mol Pb
0.0025 mol Pb^{2+} + 0.005 mol e^- (0.005 F) $\rightarrow$ 0.0025 mol Pb

$m = nM = 0.0025$ mol $\times$ 207 g mol^{-1} Pb
$\qquad = 0.5175$ g Pb
2 mol $Br^- \rightarrow 1$ mol Br_2 + 2 mol e^-(2F)
0.005 mol $Br^- \rightarrow 0.0025$ mol Br_2 + 0.005 mol e^-(0.005 F)

$V = nV_m = 0.0025$ mol $\times$ 22.4 dm^3 mol^{-1} Br_2
$\qquad = 0.056$ dm^3 Br_2

CHAPTER 16.
AN INTRODUCTION
TO ORGANIC
CHEMISTRY

(8)

Volume of hydrocarbon	$= 20\ cm^3$
Volume of total oxygen	$= 200\ cm^3$
Volume of carbon dioxide	
and excess oxygen	$= 150\ cm^3$
Volume of excess oxygen	$= 50\ cm^3$
Volume of carbon dioxide	$= 150\ cm^3 - 50\ cm^3 = 100\ cm^3$
Volume of oxygen used	$= 200\ cm^3 - 50\ cm^3 = 150\ cm^3$

$$C_xH_y + \left(x + \frac{y}{4}\right)O_2 \rightarrow xCO_2 + \frac{y}{4}H_2O$$

$20\ cm^3 \qquad 150\ cm^3 \quad 100\ cm^3$

In accordance with Avogadro's hypothesis, we can substitute moles for volumes

$$C_xH_y + \left(x + \frac{y}{4}\right)O_2 \rightarrow xCO_2 + \frac{y}{4}H_2O$$

$20\ mol \qquad 150\ mol \quad 100\ mol$

Dividing each by 20

$$C_xH_y + \left(x + \frac{y}{4}\right)O_2 \rightarrow xCO_2 + \frac{y}{4}H_2O$$

$1\ mol \qquad \frac{15}{2}\ mol \quad 5\ mol$

Since x mol $CO_2 = 5$ mol then $x = 5$
and $(x + y/4)$ mol $= \frac{15}{2}$ mol
then $(5 + y/4)$ mol $= \frac{15}{2}$ mol then $y = 10$

Therefore, the empirical formula of the hydrocarbon, C_xH_y, is C_5H_{10}

(9)

Constituent	C	H
Mass/g	18.26	1.74
Molar mass/g mol^{-1}	12.0	1.0
Amount/mol	1.52	1.74
$\dfrac{\text{Amount}}{\text{Smallest amount}}$	1	1.14
Simplest ratio	7	8

Empirical formula $= C_7H_8$

Molecular formula $= (\text{Empirical formula})_n$
$$= (C_7H_8)_n$$
$$= (7 \times 12 + 8 \times 1)_n$$
$$92 = 92n$$
$$n = 1$$

Molecular formula $= C_7H_8$

(10)

Volume of hydrocarbon $= 30 \text{ cm}^3$
Volume of total oxygen $= 120 \text{ cm}^3$
Volume of carbon dioxide
and excess oxygen $= 90 \text{ cm}^3$
Volume of excess oxygen $= 30 \text{ cm}^3$
Volume of carbon dioxide $= 90 \text{ cm}^3 - 30 \text{ cm}^3 = 60 \text{ cm}^3$
Volume of oxygen used $= 120 \text{ cm}^3 - 30 \text{ cm}^3 = 90 \text{ cm}^3$

$$C_xH_y + \left(x + \frac{y}{4}\right)O_2 \rightarrow xCO_2 + \frac{y}{4}H_2O$$
$$30 \text{ cm}^3 \qquad 90 \text{ cm}^3 \quad 60 \text{ cm}^3$$

In accordance with Avogadro's hypothesis, we can substitute moles for volumes

$$C_xH_y + \left(x + \frac{y}{4}\right)O_2 \rightarrow xCO_2 + \frac{y}{4}H_2O$$
$$30 \text{ mol} \qquad 90 \text{ mol} \quad 60 \text{ mol}$$

Dividing each by 30

$$C_xH_y + \left(x + \frac{y}{4}\right)O_2 \rightarrow xCO_2 + \frac{y}{4}H_2O$$
$$1 \text{ mol} \qquad 3 \text{ mol} \quad 2 \text{ mol}$$

Since x mol $CO_2 = 2$ mol then $x = 2$
and $(x + y/4)$ mol $= 3$ mol
then $(5 + y/4)$mol $= 3$ mol then $y = 4$

Therefore, the empirical formula of the hydrocarbon, C_xH_y, is C_2H_4.

CHAPTER 20. ALIPHATIC CARBOXYLIC ACIDS AND ESTERS

(12)

(e)

$CH_3OH + CH_3COOH \rightarrow CH_3COOCH_3 + H_2O$
1 mol CH_3OH reacts with 1 mol CH_3COOH
Mass of methanol, $m = V \times d = 5 \text{ cm}^3 \times 0.8 \text{ g cm}^{-3} = 4.0 \text{ g}$

Mass of ethanoic acid, $m = V \times d = 5 \text{ cm}^3 \times 1.0 \text{ g cm}^{-3} = 5.0 \text{ g}$

Amount of CH_3OH, $n = \dfrac{m}{M} = \dfrac{4.0 \text{ g}}{32 \text{ g mol}^{-1}} = 0.125 \text{ mol } CH_3OH$

Amount of CH_3COOH,

$$n = \frac{m}{M} = \frac{5.0 \text{ g}}{60 \text{ g mol}^{-1}} = 0.0833 \text{ mol } CH_3COOH$$

As 0.125 mol > 0.0833 mol, then CH_3COOH is the limiting reactant.

(f)
Actual mass of methyl ethanoate obtained
Mass of methyl ethanoate, $m = V \times d = 4.8 \text{ cm}^3 \times 0.9 \text{ g cm}^{-3} = 4.32 \text{ g}$

Theoretical mass of methyl ethanoate obtained

$CH_3OH + CH_3COOH \rightarrow CH_3COOCH_3 + H_2O$
0.0833 mol $CH_3COOH \rightarrow 0.0833$ mol CH_3COOCH_3

0.0833 mol $CH_3COOCH_3 = 0.0833 \text{ mol} \times 74 \text{ g mol}^{-1} CH_3COOCH_3$
$= 6.16 \text{ g } CH_3COOCH_3$

$$\% \text{ Yield} = \frac{\text{Actual yield}}{\text{Theoretical yield}} \times 100\% = \frac{4.32}{6.16} \times 100\%$$

$$= 70\%$$